"Cookie" Fetterman

Tree of Life by David Revak

Like My New Shoes?

David and Blairanne Revak

LifeGuides Press

My Life © 2012 by David Revak revised to become
Like My New Shoes? © 2016 by Blair and David Revak

Palatino ~ David's voice
Comic sans ~Blair's voice

No portion of this book may be reproduced
in any way without express written consent of author

Published by
LifeGuides Press
Mesa, AZ 85209
480 703-1244

David's Dedication

This book is dedicated to

Blairanne

Blairanne's Dedication

And now as my David has left me
May I dedicate this book to Us.
David and Blairanne
And a wonderful Revak family of
children, grandchildren and great-grandchildren.
April 2016
May we all share the hugely wonderful life of the Revak Family.

Table of Contents

Prologue		Blair
CHAPTER 1	David's Background	David
CHAPTER 2	Mt Carmel	David
CHAPTER 3	Cornell	David
CHAPTER 4	Dearest David	Blair
CHAPTER 5	Blairanne	Blair
CHAPTER 6	We Meet	David
CHAPTER 7	HEATHER	Blair
CHAPTER 8	Began Internship	David & Blair
CHAPTER 9	MATTHEW	Blair
CHAPTER 10a	Practice in Bloomsburg	David
CHAPTER 10b	SHALLY	Blair
CHAPTER 10c	More About Practice in Bloomsburg	David
CHAPTER 11	Crownpoint	David & Blair
CHAPTER 12	Return to Bloomsburg	David
CHAPTER 13	CELESTIA	Blair
CHAPTER 14	CHARLES	Blair
CHAPTER 15	Yeah, Its Cancer	David & Blair
CHAPTER 16	Winding up the Practice	David
CHAPTER 17	Retirement	David
CHAPTER 18	If I were to live my life over	David
CHAPTER 19	Cancer comes again	Blair
CHAPTER 20	Closing Thoughts	Blair

David Revak
about five years old

PROLOGUE

BLAIR ...
This is for you, our dear friends, family, and all of you who care and know about the David and Blairanne Revak family. When David was 70 I gave him the gift of a life story written in collaboration with the "Life Story Lady", Dee Dees. David and Dee met for hours and hours talking, recording and dictating David's life story. He did not complete the book, as he said, "then I'll have to die." So when he did die, Dee said to me, "You complete your story and we will finalize David's life story."

And then I thought, "will I have to die?"

I am now teetering up to the 73-year-old bar. An unbelievable milestone, considering I remember when I thought I would not live to be 40. And as I write this life story I am in the throes of grieving the loss of my David. Can I believe he is gone? No. I still insist he come back, even for a short visit. That finality is a finality that slams the door shut on my psyche.

I have not dealt with many issues of finality. There has always been the chance to review and revive. But here I am still struggling with the finality of David's departure. And I have that heavy box they say is full of his ashes. "Ashes?" I say. "Maybe ashes and titanium metal knees." I cannot believe it is so heavy. And I have not had the courage to look inside. It is packed away in the cupboard in the kitchen in the box the Neptune Society gave me. We made final cremation arrangements together soon after his diagnosis. While planning both of our cremations and death-related information, we shared some information about our end-of-life and celebration-of-life choices.

The planning involved a book with information to pass on to our survivors; including music we chose for our final services. When will I have the courage to complete mine? I don't know. David filled out only a small part of his, including the organizations to donate to and the music for his service. He listed Wounded Warriors, Hospice and Banner MD Anderson as his choices. And his songs were "Knock, Knock, Knocking on Heaven's Door" and "You're Innocent When You Dream" by Tom Wait from the movie Smoke. He had listened often to the Knock Knock Knocking song when he was in treatment for his Hodgkins Disease in 1990.

David wrote chapters as timelines of birth, childhood and adult. I will let his story stand as he presented it. And when, in his story, he tells about meeting me, I will introduce my story. And after you learn about me and I reach the time when I met him, I will go back to his story of our lives together.

I will introduce separate stories about our five children. For certainty of clarification I am using some of David's "famous" quotations as an introduction to each of our five kids. Charles collected his quotations and published them for David on his 65th birthday.

I will close with a chapter about the last two years of our time as "we". Even now, over two years after his death I find the exhaustion of the grief mounts as I write a page about him and try to compile and weave together our story.

And of course, I will write our final chapter.

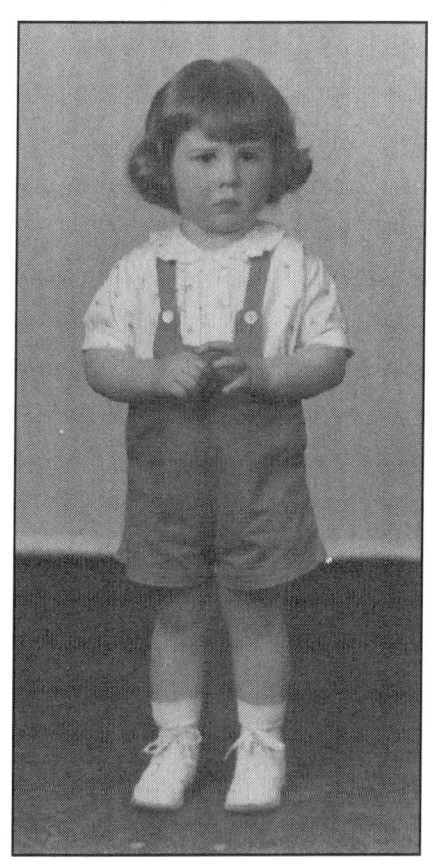

David, About two years old

Chapter 1
David's Background

DAVID …
The Revaks
Early on a rainy morning, Anna Revak gave birth to a ten-pound baby boy. By that time—May 12, 1940—the Revaks had been in the United States for about fifty years. My paternal grandfather, Wasil Revak, was one of nine brothers who came over from the Austro-Hungarian Empire and settled in Pennsylvania. A tenth brother went to Canada first, later arriving in the US illegally. The Revaks made their living as farmers and miners.

Granddad Revak married Anna Matsko, who was also a recent immigrant. Her oldest brother had brought Anna and several of her brothers into the country around 1904, when she was about 14 years old. Anna must have met and married Wasil Revak very soon afterward, because by 1908, when she was just 18, she already had three children—my dad, John, being her third. Another daughter would be born in 1913, before tragedy struck.

In 1914, 29-year-old Wasil was killed in a mining accident, leaving a 24-year-old widow with four children under the age of 10. Grandma began taking in boarders to provide an income for her family, and in 1917 she became pregnant by one of her boarders, resulting in the birth of her son Paul.

The boarding house proved to be fertile grounds, as one of Anna's daughters, Tatiana (Tilly), became pregnant by another renter, and gave birth to Walter in 1925. Anna raised that grandson as her own child, which made for some confusing relationships. Grandma Anna later married a miner named Anthony Berezovski, and had another daughter she named Pearl.

Dad

My Dad, John Walter Revak, was born in 1908 and grew up in Mt. Carmel Township, PA. He was only six when his father died in the mining accident, and so Dad had a rough childhood. His mother and sister both became pregnant from boarders, and so he had two more "brothers;" one of whom (Paul) was a half-brother, and the other (Walter) was actually a nephew.

When Dad was just thirteen he began doing janitorial work at the newspaper office—cleaning bathrooms and spittoons—and he had his first sexual experience … in a whorehouse. At that time in Mt. Carmel there were three "houses of ill-repute," and the term "minimum age" didn't mean much. Even in the local saloons, if you could reach the bar with a nickel, you could get a schooner of beer.

While still in his teens, Dad went to work at Homiak's Bar and Grill, which was owned by the father of his friend

George Homiak. When Prohibition closed the bar down in the 1920s, Dad was suddenly involved in bootlegging. Homiak's was only a few hundred yards away from the brewery for Anthracite beer. Workers—who seemed to be digging harmless trenches—were actually laying pipes that would connect the brewery to the garage at Homiak's bar. The guys in the brewery were still making beer in the basement, which would be bottled and transferred to the bar's garage—a speakeasy where people came to drink. The beer would be shipped to other places as well.

Even though the Volstead Act prohibited the sale of alcohol, the federal government didn't do much to enforce it. In fact, according to Dad, the investigators—mostly single guys with the federal government—were on the take. Everyone was paid off with women, booze, cigarettes, and money. They came in supposedly to check for illegal sales of alcohol, but in reality, they drank beer and went to the whorehouse. They made out pretty well, getting a government salary and bootleg money as well. That activity was common back then. Dad said a lot of people were pissed when prohibition was repealed. The bootleggers were making more money with the illegal beer, and the government men were getting double pay.

While prohibition was questionably successful in reducing the amount of alcohol sold and consumed, it had the adverse effect of increasing other illegal activities; bootlegging, underground sales, and organized crime. The law was finally repealed in 1933.

Dad had very little formal education, having quit school after the eighth grade, but he earned his GED later on. He was often heard to say, "A little education is a dangerous thing."

He was also quite a ladies man and remained a bachelor until he was about 29 years old. Part of his charm was due to his being a great dancer, having mastered the polka, ballroom dancing and others. It was at a dance that he met my mother.

The Zelez's (Jelus)
My maternal grandparents were also immigrants. Grandfather John Zelez was born in 1886 and had emigrated from Slovakia—also in the Austro-Hungarian Empire—to the US sometime before 1900. The genealogy states it was 1900, but one daughter was born in Mt. Carmel, PA in 1896, so it had to have been before that. Like my other grandfather, John was also a miner, and died of lung disease in 1946. After his first wife died, he married again and had a second family.

My maternal grandmother, Anna Hanzsush, was born in 1886, also in Slovakia. "Baba," as I called her, was an angry woman. When I was in high school, I asked Mom why Baba was always so angry. She told me that Baba had been brought to America as an indentured servant to a family of lawyers. She and her sister were badly used, being passed around from one boy to another in the family.

It's thought that she arrived here around 1900. We don't know when she married, or when her first three children were born, but her fourth was born in 1910. My mother—the sixth child—was born in 1915, and her youngest of eight was born in 1928. That's well over 20 years of child-bearing!

Mom - Anna Jelus

Mom—yet another Anna—was born Anna Jelus, in Pennsylvania, December 1915. After my grandfather Zelez arrived in the States, the name was changed slightly to Jelus. Mom had wanted to become a nurse, but was told by her mother, "We only educate the boys."

Mom also carried a lot of repressed anger. Maybe it was being told only the boys would be educated, or maybe she wished she were a man and could have the same chances in life. I would later learn more about what caused her anger.

I don't know much about her childhood, other than that she was a good basketball player. She graduated from high school during the Depression, when few could afford a class yearbook. I know she liked to dance. When she met the handsome, charming, John Revak at a dance, he swept her off her feet … and then got her pregnant. His mother insisted he marry Anna. They never celebrated wedding anniversaries, and to this day I don't know the date of their marriage. In December of 1938 my brother Tom was born, and I came along a year and a half later.

I once told Tom, during one of our frequent brotherly fights, that it was his fault that Mom and Dad had to get married, because she was pregnant with him. He became very angry at me, and I'm not sure he ever forgave me for the comment.

Family Life

Growing up in that household was extremely stressful. Our parents existed in a contentious relationship on and off for over fifty years, probably because they resented being forced into marriage. There was always some violence and duplicity in the household as they fought over everything: money, religion, drinking, and anything else that might come up.

Dad's irresponsibility with money was one of the biggest issues between the two of them. Bill collectors were constantly after him, and Mom cried all the time from the stress and humiliation of it all. When she'd finally had enough, she stood up to Dad, demanding that she take over responsibility for the finances. However, the stress of constantly worrying about money took its toll, and she became a closet drinker; creating yet another issue to quarrel about.

They also fought over religion. Dad was Russian Orthodox, and Mom was originally Slovak Lutheran before joining the Hungarian Reform Church with her father. My brother, Tom, attended the Russian Orthodox church where he served as an alter boy. I, on the other hand, attended the United Church of Christ with my mother, and was not even baptized until I was twelve. This was very confusing—and hurtful—to me, and wasn't explained until later.

My mom was studying Russian faith lessons when Tom was taken to be baptized at St. Michael's Russian Orthodox church. The priest told her that since she wasn't a member yet, Tom could not be baptized inside the church, but would be baptized outside on the front steps. Mom was furious and said, "No son of mine will ever be baptized here!" which was why I wasn't baptized until I was twelve, prior to confirmation.

The constant fighting, especially over money and religion had a profound—and ultimately positive—effect on me. I hated seeing Mom so unhappy, constantly crying, and worrying over the bills. I resolved at an early age that I would never be irresponsible with my finances. I didn't want to live with bill collectors chasing me, and I would never put my family through that kind of stress. I vowed that no way in hell would anyone ever hassle me because I didn't have money or the means to protect what I owned.

As for religion, I was determined that if I ever got married, I would convert to my wife's faith, and I would practice it. I considered myself an agnostic at the time, but knew I would do whatever was necessary to avoid fighting over religion.

Our family was not one to show affection, since Dad and Mom were perpetually angry at one another. Tom and I knew our mother loved us, but she was emotionally cold, offering no hugs, touching, or affection of any kind.

However she was a good mother, and demonstrated her love in other ways. She always encouraged us in our ventures, took us to concerts, and provided intellectual stimulation. She made sure we had good books and encouraged reading. That was her style of love. Still, it was tough being a kid in that household.

Mom's own family life had not been easy, either. Most of her brothers were alcoholics, and the youngest, Albert, was stricken with tuberculosis. He lived with us for a short time and Mom took care of him. All of that, plus being in a loveless marriage, took its toll on her.

Dad's social face was quite different from his home persona. At home he could be angry and gruff. But away from home he was charming and a joy to be around. He was a good entertainer, an excellent tennis player, and liked to say he could drink with "dukes and pukes" alike. And he loved to dance.

Dad didn't get along with Mom's brother and they often fought. Knives would be pulled and flashed about, and both men could become quite violent. I resented Dad's anger while I was growing up, but when we had a heart-to-heart talk in later years, I began to understand and appreciate more of what he had gone through.

He acknowledged that he hadn't been as good a father as he might have been. He said, "No one understands, I never had a dad, I had to go to work. Here I was, a young boy seven years old, who lost his father in a mine accident. My Mom was sleeping with a boarder and my sister got pregnant with another. I was taken to a whorehouse when I was 13 and didn't know what I was doing. I never had opportunities in life! How could I be a loving father when I never experienced that myself?"

After I learned more about his life and all that he had gone through, I was able to forgive his anger and appreciate what he had done for us. He may not have known how to love, but he never left us, and in his own way, he managed to provide for us. He was always supportive of Tom and me being educated, and he attended all our sporting events.

He was able to overcome his difficult childhood to become successful in his own way. Before marriage he had become an apprentice printer at the newspaper where he had started as a janitor as a young boy, and eventually became a full-fledged printer. He was very proud of the fact that he knew how to properly split words, and could read upside-down and backwards.

Dad became a union leader in industrial relations, and was continually elected president of the union, even though he didn't really want the position. But he kept the unions going, and didn't take any BS from anyone. He was also elected to the town council in Mt. Carmel. Dad was actually a very bright man who could have gone far with the right opportunities. But he always told me "Don't ever run for an elected office or get into politics, because you don't just have a closet full of skeletons … you've got a room full!"

Tom

Tom was seventeen months older than I, and a very bright and talented guy—one of those people who seemed to have everything; brains, talent, sports ability and looks. And yet he was never happy. He was a certified genius, a member of Mensa, in the National Honor Society, and listed in Who's Who. He was a wonderful pianist, a master chess player, and a sports champion who ran the Boston Marathon. Tom enjoyed studying and reading, and was first in his class in high school, which was unfortunate for me, because teachers would always compare me to him. He graduated from Cornell University and earned a medical degree from Cornell Medical School.

Tom's dream career was to become a pianist, but that wasn't something people from the small town of Mt. Carmel did, so he was angry and bitter about having that dream thwarted. When he wanted to marry the daughter of the Mayor of Montreal, her parents were against the idea, and sent her to Europe to break them up. He became more cynical and pessimistic about life.

While at Cornell Medical School, Tom met a nursing student, Floranne Hahn, and married her on June 6th, 1966. He was highly interested in numerology, and the number three was extremely important to him. So it's interesting that his wedding date was 6/6/66, using a combination of three. Three years later, Tom and Floranne had a son, Kurt.

When Tom graduated from Cornell in 1967, the Viet Nam war was in full swing. Tom volunteered and wanted to serve in the Green Berets. He had been in the ROTC at Cornell, and so was able to get a commission in the U.S. Army. He served a tour in Viet Nam, leaving the military as a Captain.

One of his military buddies from Viet Nam, Carl Bancoff, wrote a book years later, entitled *A Forgotten Man*. He sent me a copy, dedicating it to Tom. I haven't read the book, but the description on the jacket flap makes me wonder if it might have been based loosely on Tom, as several of the personality traits of the main character seemed very similar.

Along with so much talent, often comes turmoil. Tom suffered from manic-depression, and saw psychiatrists for years; one of whom called him a whirling dervish, which aptly described his chaotic lifestyle. He was excessive in his use of alcohol and prescription drugs.

Whether due to the lack of affection in his childhood, or the various disappointments in his life, Tom's pessimism ate away at him. His marriage was screwed up, but now he had a young son to care for. He had learned nothing from our father's experience with financial irresponsibility, and he too now owed money to everyone. To help dig his way out of being deep in debt, he became involved in Medicare fraud in New York, and was about to be indicted.

Eventually, all the disappointments, problems, and mental issues took their toll. On October 20, 1975, he went to a motel and took 30 pills at 3:00 a.m., (again, the threes) ending his life of turbulence. In the suicide note found in his motel room, he had written, "No. three," referring to the room number. He was only 35 years old.

His death was of course devastating to us all, and caused more rancor within the family. Because he had taken his own life, he couldn't be buried in the church. This infuriated my father; especially since Aunt Tilly, who had been a prostitute and lived a rough, immoral lifestyle, had been allowed that privilege. Dad felt it was an insult to Tom and the family, and he remained angry at the church the rest of his life.

Floranne, who had been an LPN, had mental problems of her own, and Tom's death pushed her over the edge, causing her to be institutionalized. Their son, Kurt, was only six years old when Tom died. When Floranne was taken away, my parents took Kurt in and helped raise him until his mother was once again able to take over.

I remember Tom telling me once—with his usual pessimism—"We're doomed; no matter what we do in life, we're going to fail."

I wasn't sure if he was referring to people in general, or just the two of us, but I bought into it for a while. I used to set myself up to fail, until I recognized what I was doing, and stopped. I was determined I would never raise my kids that way.

Chapter 2
Mt. Carmel

DAVID …

The small town of Mt. Carmel, Pennsylvania, where I grew up, had a population of about 8,000, encompassing a wide variety of ethnic groups. The Welsh ran the mines, the Irish were the service workers, and the Hungarians, Polish and Slovaks were miners and did a little of everything else.

Each ethnic group had its own bar, school and church. At one time Mt Carmel was known as "The City of Churches," claiming over 20 different houses of worship in the town. Each one had its own style of bell-ringing, and by listening, you knew which church was calling its flock. Despite all the churches, the little village also hosted three whorehouses.

The Anthracite Brewing Company—later called the Mt. Carmel Brewery—had been a staple in the town since 1897, until it closed in 1951; about the same time the mining "boom" began to decline.

Mt. Carmel was not a bad place to grow up. The Revaks had farms in nearby Trevorton, and I had plenty of cousins, so there was always someone to play with, and fun places to do it. We only lived about 15 miles apart so it was easy to get together. No one was worried about being "politically correct" back then, and every ethnic group would tease the others mercilessly. We kidded around, we fought, and we made up.

I was close to most of my cousins while growing up, and followed their paths as adults. One became vice-president of a bank, one attended West Point and went into the military, others became lawyers, engineers, doctors or dentists. And one went to jail for armed robbery. No family is perfect. But most of us are sober, successful, and religious.

A couple of other relatives were always in and out of our lives. My dad's sister Tatiana, whom we called Tilly, was one of those. She became pregnant at fourteen and had a son by a boarder who lived in her mother's house. Her mother, Anna, raised the boy as her own.

Tilly was a bit eccentric, and had an interesting—if not always moral—lifestyle. She had at one time been a prostitute and a madam. I always wondered how she got into that, but never wanted to ask. She had been young, with no education, and it may have been a survival strategy. Later in life she lived on welfare.

Dad told us that Tilly had witnessed a murder at one of the whorehouses in New York City. The police wanted her to testify, but the mob was after her, so she hid out somewhere until things cooled down. She later met and married Henry Lane, and had four children by him.

We called Tilly the "Monkey Lady," because of her penchant for keeping monkeys in Mt. Carmel. She had a dozen or more tiny monkeys in a very large cage. They were cute little things, and when she'd let them out of the cage, they'd scamper all over, and climb across your shoulders and onto your head. Usually, they were fun, but when they got angry, they'd throw their poop at you. Aunt Tilly may have been eccentric, but she was a good, kind person, and I always liked her.

When—in her eighties—she was dying of terminal bowel cancer, I took care of her at a nursing home in Bloomsburg. When I went to see her during her first weeks there, I asked how she was doing. She said, "David—there's not a good fuck in the whole place."

Uncle Albert is another who was a big part of our lives. Albert Lindbergh Jelus was born the year after Charles Lindbergh made his famous flight—which explains the middle name. He was my mother's youngest brother, and, while her other brothers were rough alcoholics, Uncle Albert was one of the nicest, kindest, most gentle men I ever knew. He was a fancy dresser, and a real sweetheart of a guy.

He contracted tuberculosis and stayed with us for a while. We all took care of him, and Tom and I had to help him to the bathroom, and help care for him in general.

My parents talked about Uncle Albert having a girlfriend, but no one ever came to see him when he was sick, which Tom and I thought was strange. He may have been gay, but it was never mentioned, and there would be no way to prove it. He never married, and I don't remember ever seeing him with lady friends. The disease eventually attacked his kidneys, and he died from TB and kidney failure in 1955, at home in Mt. Carmel.

I'm sure I became positive for TB while helping to care for him, but we were young and vital, and it never materialized into anything. Still, it would cause me some concern later in life when I became ill.

Except for the tension at home, I had a great childhood until I was about eight years old. Life in Mt. Carmel was good, and I was happy during those early years. My grandmother lived next door and I would often sneak over to her house for a second dinner. She took advantage of my being there to lecture me about the possibilities of becoming a bum. Many of the kids would loaf around their shanties—the little shed most folks had behind their houses—to smoke cigarettes and drink homemade booze. Grandma would start in on me; "Study, study, you have to go to college or you will be a hunky, hieky, loafa shanty bum."

My mom ran a very disciplined household; at least where Tom and I were concerned. Back then parents had high expectations for their kids, and kids did what they were told. My parents were no different. Dinner was served at a certain time, and we were expected to be there, seated at the table. We ate what was served: there were no queries as to what we would like for dinner. We went to Bible School, and were expected to do well in school. I had to be home by 9:00 p.m. on school nights and 10:30 on Saturdays ... no exceptions!

Mom was always right there while we were studying or doing homework, making sure we weren't slacking off. She'd say, "Read it again. Do it again. Read it to me."

"But Mom, why do I have to read it over and over again?"

"Repetition is the mother of learning," she would say.

That lesson stayed with me all my life. I repeated it to my kids as they were growing up, and my teacher daughter now repeats it to the kids in her classroom!

I actually enjoyed school as a kid, and always liked learning new things. I attended kindergarten at Garfield School, and started first grade at McKinley in 1946. I was nice looking, thin, fun to be around, and everybody liked me. I loved going to movies, and had dreams of being an actor.

I was quick to memorize lines, and was selected to perform in a Bible school skit. I still remember my lines …

"I come from the quarry and I am the rock

I'll build a foundation to stand any shock

So use me good builder if you would be sure

To make a foundation that ere will endure."

There were kids from another Sunday School seated in the front row, and as I said my verse, they began to laugh and make fun of me. That triggered my reluctance to speak before a group, and I swore then that I would never be in another play.

By the time I was twelve, I had begun to overeat to compensate for all the turmoil in the house, and began putting on weight. Naturally, the other kids would pick on me because I couldn't run as fast, and wasn't as good at games.

By the time I got to Roosevelt Jr. High in 1952, I had a lot of anger. My adolescent years were pretty traumatic, as I guess they are for many kids. But there was so much hostility in our home, that I couldn't help carry some around with me. Most kids seemed to like me, and I couldn't understand why, because I didn't like myself. I was chubby, wore glasses, and had unstylishly short hair.

Despite my popularity with most of the kids, there were still bullies picking on me and making my life miserable; calling me four-eyes, fat boy, and other hurtful names. One kid harassed me continually through seventh and eighth grades, usually with a hard slap on the back of the head, or "titty twisting." No one ever came to my defense.

I'd go home and tell Dad, and he'd just say "You've got to stand up to those kids; strike back. I can't go down there and fight your fights. It's between you and them. If you catch them, punch them in the stomach and knock the wind out them. They'll stop once they know you'll fight back."

I wanted to follow his advice, but I could never catch them. I would give chase, but they could always run faster because I was heavy.

After a while of this, I'd had enough. During the summer between eighth and ninth grades, I began my own workout program to get in shape. I started getting up at five a.m. and running along the railroad tracks; sometimes along the banks of coal, sometimes on the ties, and even on the rails themselves. I got to where I could run 30 or 40 feet right on the narrow rails. At first I'd lift rocks for weights to build my arm muscles, and then I became friends with a kid who had weights. We'd refer to the Joe Atlas body-building manual, and lift weights every day. I continued this through the summer months, and got strong and lean.

When I returned to ninth grade in the fall, I was ready. The first time the kid slapped me on the back of the head, I took off after him, caught him, and beat the living shit out of him. I just kept pummeling away until we were pulled apart.

I was sent to the office, and the kid I had clobbered came in with his mother, who wanted me expelled from school. The principal said, "I'll deal with Davey Revak, but your son and others have been picking on him for the last couple of years. Your son got what he deserved."

I fully expected to get a few whacks from the paddle, as I had on previous occasions, but this time the principal just said "Don't let this happen again … I want to see you out for football."

That same summer, I was able to attend a shop class taught by Mr. Sheetz. I chose to build a cedar chest, and was looking forward to presenting it to my mom. Every morning I'd go to the shop from 9:00 to 12:00 and work under his guidance. I built the chest, gave it a coat of shellac, and hammered copper plates for the hinges and fittings. It was coming right along.

Then it was time for football practice to begin. The principal had said he wanted me to go out for it, and I was thinking seriously about it, primarily because I didn't feel he was giving me an option.

Unfortunately, practice time conflicted with shop class, so I had a dilemma. As we were putting the finishing touches on the cedar chest, I told Mr. Sheetz that I needed to begin football practice. He responded, "Mr. Revak, you'd better show up here. If you don't, and I find out you went to football practice, you won't be allowed to keep the cedar chest. I'll sell it."

I stormed toward the door at the other end of the room, with classmates watching. All I could think about was that I'd worked so hard on the cedar chest, and now wouldn't be able to give it to my mom. My anger and temper overcoming good sense, I turned around and said, "Mr. Sheetz?"

"What?" he asked.

"Stick the cedar chest up your ass!"

He flew across the room after me, and I was out the door and running like the dickens. He chased me for more than two blocks, yelling "Mr Revak, this is not over!"

When my mother found out what had happened, she made me write a letter of apology. Dad said, "You've got to respect the teachers. They're not there to take your baloney. You learn everything you can."

I started football practice, and on the first day of school, I had shop class. Mom had told me to go to Mr. Sheetz and apologize to him personally. All he said was, "We used to be friends."

I was caught in the middle, because I'd practically been ordered to try out for football by Mr. Dallabrida, who was not only the principal, but also my football line coach. Luckily, he and Dad were good friends, so Mom, Dad and I told him the cedar chest story, then they all talked to Mr. Sheetz. He had not sold the cedar chest, and finally gave his consent for me to have it. We did not own a car, but Dad borrowed one so we could pick up the chest and deliver it home.

I was a good boy that year; I didn't say anything I shouldn't have, and I made the honor roll every time. But Mr. Sheetz never forgave me. At graduation I thanked him again for giving me the chest, but he just turned and walked away.

So I played football. I started on the freshman football team and played on the varsity practice team until the season started. Then I joined the wrestling team. Most Mt. Carmel students were expected to be involved in sports in some way. The boys would go out for various teams, and the girls would be the cheerleaders, since there wasn't enough funding to support girl's teams.

Still, Mt. Carmel had a good record. Around that time, 1954-55, we were Eastern Conference champions, and third in the nation in terms of number of games won. Later, we won the state championship every other year for about ten years, during the 1990s until about 2001.

I had gone out for football in eighth grade, but wasn't doing well in my studies that first semester. Mom wasn't happy about that, and put an end to after-school football practice. She made me sit and do my homework and study, saying "If you have to sit here until you graduate high school, you're gonna get a good report card."

I was smart and could do the work, so I buckled down and got it done. As long as I made the honor roll, I was allowed to play sports in ninth grade. I was one of only two or three freshmen on the team that year.

I liked wrestling, but was still a little chubby when I started, and couldn't win the first year—in fact, I ended the year at 0 and 14. During that freshman year, I experienced a humiliating defeat. I wrestled a district champ who would let me escape rather than pin me, piling up the points to 18-0. Then he pinned me in the final seconds of the match. I yelled, "You son-of-a-bitch!"

During the next couple of years I remembered that incident and felt the need to get even when I met a kid from the same school. I won a few matches my sophomore year, and was undefeated my senior year.

Tom had naturally been an excellent student, and a star football player ... and I was always living in his shadow. When football practice began, the coach said, "If you're only half as good as your brother, you'll be a great addition to Cornell."

He thought he was paying me a compliment. I interpreted it as understanding that I would never be recognized as me. Even in the classroom, Tom's excellence was always held up to me. I once challenged my senior

English teacher—also wife of the principal—on a topic, and she told me that I always got by off the reputation of my brother.

The stigma of always being unfavorably compared to Tom, along with the trauma of being laughed at while performing in Bible school, were always in the back of my mind. Ironically, it wasn't until after Tom died that I finally felt I could move forward and begin to live my own life. Even the fear of public speaking left me.

By high school I had leaned out, was feeling fit, and having fun. I had been chosen prom king and class president, and was dating my first love; a Portuguese-Italian girl. We went together for about a year and a half before she threw me over for a state wrestling champ.

I was getting lots of well-deserved advice from Mom and Dad about dating. When I'd go out, Mother would say "Just remember, love is blind, but the neighbors aren't. They are out there watching everything."

It was true; in fact, one of our neighbors, Mr. Stein, never spoke to us, but he would go into his former outhouse—now used as a storage room—and hide there, listening to the activity in his neighbor's yards.

Dad's advice to me was more blunt: "If you get a hard-on, you don't put it anywhere except a window sill; then let the window drop on it."

Then he would point to his crotch and say "If you're going to use this, be sure you use this," moving his pointing finger toward his head.

He would also tell me, "You can go out on Saturday night and raise hell, but you'd better get up and go to church on Sunday. No excuses! I'll throw you out of bed myself!" The threat was real, but he never followed through with it.

I was a good student and made the Honor Society, and continued to be active in sports throughout high school. I ran track, was captain of the wrestling team, and football co-captain during my senior year. I won lots of awards—including the Babe Ruth Award—and I was voted most popular male. A quotation under my picture in the yearbook read, "He needs no verse to fame him, merit true doth name him."

Yet, somehow ... I never felt I deserved any of it.

Tom and David as teens

High School Yearbook listing

Chapter 3
Cornell

DAVID ...

Tom was already a sophomore at Cornell University when I started my freshman year there in 1958. I would have preferred another school, but my parents wanted me to attend Cornell, and I had earned a scholarship there, so that's where I went.

I had gotten into sports early in life, and did well, because I still had that anger. I wrestled to hurt as well as to win. And I was just as aggressive in playing football, which proved to be a mistake, as I blew out my left knee during a game the next semester.

I couldn't play football and I wasn't happy, so—after just a year and a half—I dropped out of Cornell in January of 1960, blowing a twenty-thousand-dollar scholarship; a full ride.

After leaving Cornell, I spent three months working on a garbage truck for the borough, which mortified my mother. In April I went to New Jersey to work for Ford Motor Company, while I applied to other schools. By June I had signed up for a six-week summer course at University of Pennsylvania, quitting my job with Ford after just two months. While at U of PA that summer, I also practiced with the football team. When I wanted to go back to Ford in the fall, with a brace, the boss didn't want to take chance on hiring me again.

I found work at a sheet metal place for a short time in the fall of 1960, until I was hired on at Delco Remy, in the battery division. We wore big gloves and had to take battery plates off and transfer them to a conveyer belt while they were cooling. I lifted about 20 tons of cooling plates onto a stack each day. It was a job everyone had to start with, but I was fit and in shape.

Around Easter, 1961, I was laid off from Delco. A buddy, Ralph Marsh had just bought a 1958 Chevy convertible, and said "Let's go to Florida with Richard Guyans."

So we headed south. Our timing wasn't the best, as there were student riots going on in Florida during spring break. We were in Ft. Lauderdale about a month, staying with some guys from the University of Miami. When we went back to New Jersey, I didn't contact my parents for almost three months, just out of anger and stubbornness. When I finally did see them, Dad asked why I couldn't call. Then he said something I've always remembered … "When you were young, you danced around my knees, now you dance around my heart."

I had always had a job, even while going to school, but in the summer of '61 I was out of work. I didn't want to go back to the sheet metal place, and Ford wouldn't hire me back, so I went to Johns-Manville, and worked there on and off about a year and a half. At the same time, I worked three hours a day stocking shelves, and put in about 20 hours on weekends.

I was living with my friend Ralph, who was a high school wrestling mate and fellow graduate from Mt. Carmel. He now lives in Show Low, Arizona, and recently retired from the post office. We continue that friendship.

We worked the 3:00 to 11:00 p.m. shift at Johns-Manville, and then we'd go to the same bar every night and drink. When they closed at 1:00 a.m., we'd go to the next county to drink until 3:00 a.m., and yet another to drink until 5:00 a.m. We'd finally drag ourselves home to sleep until it was time for work again. How we survived the heavy drinking and long hours, I'll never know.

We were supposed to wear a mask while working, but most didn't because we couldn't talk with the mask on. Some of my buddies later sued the company after becoming ill with Mesothelioma. They got a good settlement, but I didn't get involved in that.

In the winter of 1961, I was still trying to figure out what to do with my life. I was in a bar in Mt. Carmel when coach Bob Pittello from Susquehanna University dropped in. Impressed by my size, I guess, he invited me to try out for football. I went to Susquehanna to practice with the team, made it, and was offered a scholarship. I was then told that I was ineligible to play football my first year, so I paid for school myself.

That fall I transferred to Susquehanna, and majored in Business and Accounting, and Business Relations. For the first year, I commuted the 25 miles with two veterans from the Korean war, who were a few years older than I. They were already juniors or seniors, and one was married with kids. Both of them graduated and interned at Price-Waterhouse, and both became millionaires. They eventually started their own accounting firm, and went on to form a chain of offices.

We would leave about seven in the morning and return around five that evening. I only had classes for 15 hours a week, but I spent 40 hours a week at school. This was a blessing, since I was able to study and do homework during the down time. I did well academically that year.

I had been promised a scholarship at Susquehanna, so went back the following year and played football for them, before blowing out my right knee. When the scholarship failed to materialize, I took out a loan to pay my tuition for the next two and a half years.

I always worked nights while in college—

often two jobs. And I always had money. Living with constant money problems as a child taught me to be frugal with what I had. I arranged to have a $25 savings bond taken out of my pay check every two weeks for three and a half years.

I was once again looking for work, and found a job at the Governor Snyder hotel, where I tended bar by night, and cleaned the bar and restrooms in the morning. The job included room and board, and I soon became friends with Grace, who was the hotel cook. She was a pleasant, older, divorcee with two kids, and she always gave me a good breakfast and sent me off with a bag for lunch.

In the summer of 1963, Dad, through political connections, got me a job at the Selinsgrove State School and Hospital. This facility handled mentally challenged, handicapped, and delinquent individuals.

The supervisors weeded out the employees who couldn't handle the work by putting us in a ward that housed 20-year-old kids with severe disabilities, hydrocephalous, low IQ, and other traumatic conditions. My job was to mop, clean up the ward, and give the kids their medicines. Not only did I make the cut, I discovered I was good at working with these boys. The job was fulfilling, but emotionally draining.

I wasn't getting much rest during this time. I was taking summer courses in psychology, anthropology, faith, and ethics, while working at the state school, and still working and living at the Governor Snyder Hotel. Every day I'd come home from the hospital and immediately throw my clothes in the washer. Then I'd have to mop the hotel floors before I could go up to my room and sleep for a couple of hours. I continued working there throughout my junior year.

At this point I was still a business major. I had started Cornell studying industrial labor relations, then switched to accounting at Susquehanna, and enjoyed that. Now, in my third year, I was taking business law along with more accounting, and I planned to take science courses the next year.

But I began to realize I might have talent in another area, as the kids at the state school were responding positively to me. I had developed a rapport with them; I could get them to take their medicines; and more importantly, I liked working with them. The other hospital employees would say, "You're like the Pied Piper; wherever you go, they follow."

It didn't hurt that I brought in treats. On my way into work I'd stop off at a little grocery store, wearing my uniform. One day the manager asked, "Are you going to the state school?"

I told him that I worked with the severely handicapped, and he gave me their day-old pastries to take in. This became a daily routine, and soon the kids knew treats were coming. I wore cleats on my shoes, and they'd hear the "clip, clip, clip" of my coming in, and in no time, the guys would come out and start cleaning up for me. Soon I was doing my work from 11:00 p.m. until about 1:00 in the morning, and they'd do all the work for the next hour. Afterward, they got the treats. They were glad to help me out in exchange for the pastries.

D5—the detention ward—was also where all the delinquents were; the guys in lockup. We were supposed to go into the ward in twos, but I'd go by myself. I was up there one night and brought a guy with me. He said, "You're letting these guys out?"

I said, "Yeah, I let 'em out."

He asked, "Aren't you afraid?"

But I wasn't. I'd ask, "Are you guys gonna be good?" They'd swear they would be, and I'd let them out to watch TV. I could've gotten in trouble, but didn't. If I ever had a problem, I could go to these guys and say, "Tell me what's happening."

They'd usually tell me, and I would just talk to them quietly and treat them with respect. I never had a problem.

I would also go to the farm group and they knew I had treats, too. Even though these kids were patients, they worked on the farm, taking care of livestock. The school thought that work therapy was good. The kids took care of animals, raised crops, and handled other farm-related chores. It gave them something to do, and the farm helped feed the patients. It was good for everybody. One night when I arrived at the school, I was told about a boy who was going wild and had been on a rampage for two days. The other aides said, "He's tearing this place apart."

I knew this boy and he was a good kid. I went to his room, and he could hear me coming in with my cleats on. He was just sitting there, with feces all over him and everything in the room. I said, "My God, how about if I let you out, you take a shower and then we'll sit down and talk."

He agreed, and cleaned himself up, then cleaned his room and mopped it. When he was finished, I gave him something to eat, and asked, "What happened?"

He said that while he was with the farm group a couple of the guys had raped him. Before I arrived, nobody had bothered to sit down and ask him what happened; why he was acting this way. I called the night supervisor and asked him come over, then had the kid tell him what happened. The supervisor looked at me and asked, "Would you go get those guys at farm group?"

He's the boss, so I said, "Yeah, I know those guys, I'll go get'em." I took my own car; an old Dodge Ram. By the time I got to the farm, the boss had already called the supervisor there, and he had rounded up the boys. I walked over to each one, and they just looked up at me. I said, "You know why I'm here. You, you, and you, come with me."

They didn't say a word or offer any resistance. I was a big dude, 210 pounds, muscular, wore the cleats. So I took them back to the school and they ended up back in D group. I never knew what happened to them, but I'm sure the whole episode was all hushed up.

At Susquehanna University, the faculty really cared about the individual student and took an interest in each one. It was this personal attention and counseling that helped me discover I had the necessary attitude and aptitude to become a doctor, and that put me on the path to a career in the medical field.

During my junior year at Susquehanna, I had taken an interest-aptitude test administered by Drs. Philip Bossart and Warren Pirie. When I met with them to get the results, I was asked "Why are you taking business courses? Your interest aptitude says you belong in the medical field."

I was already reading Scientific American, and other science journals, so I took their word for it and decided to switch to biology and chemistry in my second semester. It was one of the best moves I ever made.

The following year, when I was a senior, I met Blairanne Hoover. She had graduated from Central High School in York, Pennsylvania, and had come directly to Susquehanna University. A model student, she was involved in campus activities, and was well-liked by her professors. Unlike me, Blair knew exactly what she wanted in life.

I, on the other hand, was somewhat of a loner, and a few years older than most of my classmates. Except for the one season of varsity football, I wasn't active on campus. I was also a bit of a non-conformist; skipping the required chapel services, working full time—which was frowned upon, and living in the Governor Snyder Hotel, which was off-limits to

S.U. students. I also wore a beard, which was considered unacceptable and an act of rebellion.

Blair and I were quite different in many ways, but once we got to know each other, we discovered we shared the same values.

We'd had some classes together before, but had never connected. She seemed cool and aloof on the surface—the "cold scientist" persona.

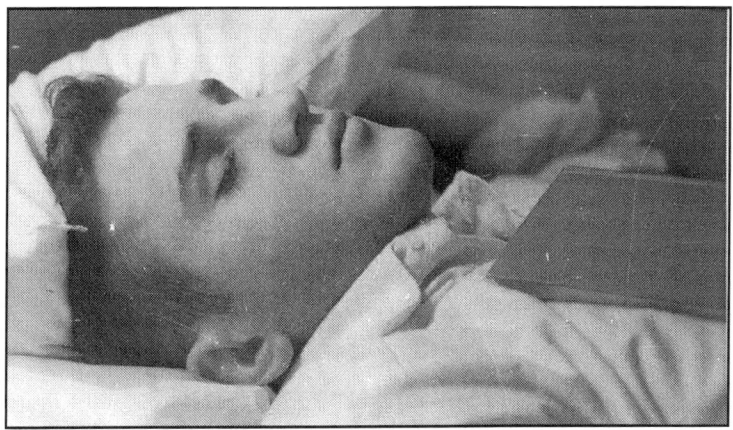

Tired from Study

Chapter 4
Dearest David

BLAIR ...

Dearest David, I've read the story of your life and I say, this is my David. But I also say, this is only a fraction of my David. And I say that with authority. I submit that forty-eight years of experience gives me a significant credential for my authority; days of laughter, days of crying, and days of asking, "Is this the day I die?"

Know what? I was often at a loss to title, to label, to anticipate your next action and your response. I might title our life together as a life of unexpected (con)sequences. Never predictable, yet always positive and loving, and always filled with a yearning to grow and share. That reminds me of the anxiety and fear I felt when I decided to marry you.

Living with a roommate for more than one semester was a struggle for me. It became boring and draining on my being. It became a burden to live with one other person. And then I wondered, how can I live for years with one man, with David, even as I love him? Could I do it? I thought maybe I could commit to three years at a time, so I opted to take the chance and marry you. And was I surprised! Life was never boring. There was always something new behind the next door.

May I add that you came from a "unique" family. For starters, I saw many old-country traditions, such as: your mom never sat down to eat with the family. Anna stood and took orders and served her men. Your Aunt Tillie, "the monkey lady," had already dazzled me with her favorite pets roaming the apartment. Your aunt who read palms had already refused to even touch my palms, never telling why. And several other aunts—observed by my untrained mind—appeared to be somewhat schizoid. What was I getting myself into? I wondered.

Should I talk to you about my life and days before you appeared in the college snack bar as an already balding football player? Let's begin with a note on our "meet and greet" experiences by sharing my plunge into romance with you. I will look back at the double helix of my life as it joined with the unique coil that is you. I will write of my life experiences as they prepared me to meet you— and for us to spend the rest of our lives together.

Our forty-seven years together were cut short when in 2014 you were taken away from me by the extensively growing esophageal cancer. Yes, we had time to prepare. You fought that valiant battle for just two weeks short of two years. And during that journey you began a career of painting. But let me go back and recount those 47 years that were a lifetime of US.

Chapter 5:
Blairanne

BLAIR ...

For me to write about myself, Blairanne, I am required to pull threads of barely visible memories of my past. I leave the past. I forget the past. In fact, I've always said, "I don't hold grudges because I can't remember what I'm supposed to be upset about." But here are those threads of memories.

John Blair Hoover was the only son born to Mae Weaver and John Addison Hoover in Brandtsville, central Pennsylvania in 1914. Four girls flanked my dad: Alma, Mary, then Dad, Anna and Miriam.

His grandfather, John Stauffer Hoover, had been a farmer, and his dad, John Addison Hoover, was a school teacher who had been active in politics and seemed to have a reputable standing in the community of Carlisle, PA. The only other Hoovers he knew about had been in the United States since the late 1700s, having migrated from the Swiss-German border. During President Herbert Hoover's time in office Grandpa was approached and told he was descended from the same family as

President Hoover. He was asked to buy a genealogy chart to find the actual lineage, but refused the offer.

Dad always reminded us of Grandpa's belief that "your word is your honor." He'd had contractual dealings of some sort and was known for his honesty. Grandpa died when I was about three years old, before I had chance to get to know him.

My cousin Mina told me that Grandpa was reputed to have had tertiary syphilis, and had been in a home of some kind with some dementia before he died. We know syphilis was not treatable until after World War 2, so he could have had it in his youth.

Grandma (Mae Weaver) Hoover lived until I was a sophomore in college at Susquehanna University. I remember her sharing stories about riding in the buggy with Grandpa when they were young and in love. She was a tiny person, always very gentle.

I remember only her declared hearing problem, which proved to be frustrating in her later years. I think she died of a stroke while in her eighties. At that time she had lived in the house many years. It wasn't the homestead Mae and John started in, nor the house where my dad grew up, but I remember it, and photos of me taken there go back to my 4-year-size child.

Beautiful lilacs blossomed every spring, and grapes grew on the large arbor just by the front door. Grandma protected the grapes from bees by wrapping small brown paper bags over the bunches.

A pitcher and bowl for washing sat by the upstairs bedroom. I don't remember using it, but I only slept over at the house one time. I do have memories of the large desk in the kitchen with lots of cubby holes in it, and of the outside toilet about 25 yards from the back door. There were posters on the walls of that toilet, behind which bees frequently nested. I was afraid to use it, so I found a space behind the outhouse where I could squat between the hollyhocks.

Aunt Mim had always lived with Grandma and never married. But when I was 12 she gave birth to Mina. The family never discussed Mina's father or anything about a relationship, although Mom told me in confidence once that she knew who Mina's father was. Mim stayed with us a while after she delivered Mina. Dad became Mina's guardian in many situations, and we always felt Mina was part of our family, though she only visited now and then. Mina and I continue in close contact to this day.

Vincanne also lived at Grandma's house. Her mom, Anna, worked as a nurse in Canandaigua, New York and, as I remember, rarely visited Grandma's house.

My mom, Annabelle Hamm, was born in 1916 to Beulah Bartolet Hamm and Levi Titus Hamm in Dillsburg, PA. She had one brother, Bill, and sisters Eleanor, Betty,

Katherine, and Jean. Levi had been previously married, so there were also a half-brother and sister.

The Dillsburg house was on Main/York Street and had a high porch nearly on the curb. It was two doors from the fire house. It had a large kitchen that took up most of the left side of the house, and a yard that went back to the alley. A garden in the back was always planted with vegetables.

I was about four years old when Grandpa and Grandma Hamm both died within one year of each other. Grandpa died in his sixties, after having a leg amputated, probably due to diabetes. Grandma died less than a year later while sitting in her rocking chair in the front room. Mom kept that rocking chair, and years later my brother Mike and his wife Peg acquired it.

My teenaged cousins, Bob and Bill, kept me at the house while everyone else went to the funeral. I don't think we visited the Hamm family much when I was a child. We did go to Dillsburg every year for the Halloween parade, which was always a treat.

Dad had been in the military as a young 17-year-old. When he graduated from high school, his father, who had some connections, sent him off with the Army to Schofield Barracks in Hawaii. Dad described his life there as being with officers and the big-wigs in the barracks. He spent his time assisting in the hospital, and returned from Hawaii matured and experienced.

He first dated my Aunt Eleanor, then met her sister Annabelle and they later married. Dad had acquired a job as a refrigeration mechanic with York Corporation, so they moved to an apartment at 105 N. Newberry Street, York, PA, about 24 miles from Dillsburg and Brandtsville.

It was common for the family to visit on Sunday afternoons. There were many cousins who shared good times together. In fact, the special vacations each year during my childhood, from 8 to 14, were a week spent in a rental beach house (within walking distance) in Stone Harbor, New Jersey. Mom began to stock cans of food and supplies in January to make possible the special trip. Other family members either shared the house or rented their own for the week.

My first Easter was a special occasion. I was 10 months old and Mom was taking me to Dillsburg to show off her new baby, dressed in full Easter regalia. It was my first long trip in a car and I became carsick on the way, creating a nauseating Easter outfit for Mom and myself. Since that day I have accrued even more embarrassing stories to share about my motion sickness experiences.

When World War 2 started Dad was drafted to serve. The two years in Hawaii didn't count toward his obligation, so he was called up again and sent to Georgia to be trained as a Medic.

Mom was pregnant with me when Dad was drafted, and I was born while he was in training in Georgia. He got a

24-hour leave to see me when I was about three months old, before he sailed on the Queen Mary to England. He came home expecting me to be named Barbara Ann. And was he surprised to find I was Blairanne. Aunt Anna had named Vincanne with the combination of her name, Ann and the man who birthed her, Vince. So Blairanne greeted Dad, and then he left for the Invasion of Normandy.

John Blair Hoover

Two years of WW2 gave Mom a time of fear and anxiety. She was alone with a new baby and under the pressure of waiting, and hoping, for her loving husband to return. The rented apartment in York backed on to the home of neighbors Katharine and Henry Bloss. When a lightning storm hit, Mom's fear prompted a trip to the Bloss residence, regardless of the hour. I later learned why she feared lightning so much. As I grew into my teens, she told me that her mother, Grandma Hamm, was struck by lightning in her house as she carried a lantern through the hall, waking all the family when a storm began. Farmers wakened and watched when a lightning storm arrived, so they could be ready in case of a fire.

Grandma survived the lightning strike, but Mom was left with a major fear. The Bloss's were special friends all our lives. Auntie Blossom, as I knew her, was a strong female influence for me. She was a Radiology Nurse and stood strong as a woman in all of her life roles. She was my go-to person for advice when I was a teen, and she encouraged and led me to strong womanhood. In fact, my high school yearbook attests to that in the caption, "… ardent Republican and women's rights advocate."

Dad's duty title is listed as "6846225, Technician Fourth Grade 634th Antiaircraft Artillery Automatic Weapons Batallion, USA." He was assigned to a professional army group and was awarded the Bronze Star medal for action at St. Vith, Belgium. He did not speak about the war for years after his return, and when he did speak, he told a few stories over again. He was on the fourth wave to land on Omaha beach in Normandy, after training in Whitby, England. Many of our men had been killed upon arrival on the beach. They determined that a 15-year-old boy was in a cave shooting, and was credited with killing a lot of American soldiers. Dad said his men refused to land with their equipment while bodies of American men were scattered all over the beach. They had to clean up the bodies before his men consented to land.

He occasionally spoke of them liberating France, the Battle of the Bulge, and the bridge at Remagen, and he often described standing at a bridge with several men who were hit and killed. Dad's uniform was shredded, but he was not hit. He was constantly checked in an attempt to understand why he was not killed. He changed guard and was missed again. He always said he was living on borrowed time as a result of his survival of multiple bombs. This may have been the occasion for the Bronze Star award. He lost a lot of his hearing there, he said.

Dad often talked about General Patton, but I can't remember anything specific. When he came home he got rid of his guns. He had enjoyed hunting as a young man, but Mom said he came home a changed man. He had to be; that was a horrific war.

I have a photo of Dad caring for a little girl during the war. He related that it was in St. Lo, France. They

Dad in St. Lo, France

set up a clinic in a church there and treated the local French people along with the American soldiers just after liberating the village. Dad never acquired the Bronze Star until our Matthew was about nine years old. When he got it, he gave it to Matthew.

In 1994 David and I toured France with the Bloomsburg High School, as chaperones and tourists. The trip included a stop at Omaha Beach and the military cemetery, and en route we stopped briefly in St. Lo. I was led to a church which still demonstrated the destruction of the war, and I took photos. Services were taking place at the time so we could not enter.

When we returned home I tried to show the photos to Dad. He said his eyes were not good enough to look at them, but after my descriptions he thought, "yes, it was the church they used."

The photo of Dad caring for the child was supposedly featured in a magazine around that time. He mentioned a military magazine. Other family members have said it was in Time or Newsweek. I keep thinking I should seek the story about this photo but have never done so. When we were in France there was a library/museum near the cemetery. I thought it may have been a good place to search, but it was closed.

The day Dad returned from the war I hid under the bed upstairs. Mom had adorned me in a pretty frock and she too had on a special dress. And I hid. When I was in my thirties and went through some hypnoanalysis, I went back to that event and described my fear. I also described the dress Mom was wearing. I later checked with Dad to see if he remembered the dress, and he said my description sounded like a dress he had purchased for Mom.

I was told that our family Doc, Dr. Shue, wanted Dad to go to Medical School to be a doctor when he returned from the war, and he offered to help him. Dad told me many years later that he had an obligation to his wife and a new child, and he chose not to do that. I am certain my choice to become a doctor relied heavily on an unconscious fulfillment of Dad's wishes.

I've often wondered why I did so want to be a doctor. Why was it that, at the age of 13, my mind was made up? I knew that the occasion of dissecting a mouse in the basement and finding babies inside was the occasion that prompted me to tell Dad, "I want to be a Doctor."

I have no memories of Dad ever encouraging me or talking to me about his experiences as a Medic in the war, or how he could see me or himself as a doctor. In fact, when I told him my plan, he quickly responded that he had to educate my younger brother Mike first, as he would be a breadwinner and needed the education. He would educate me if he could.

Shortly after returning from the war, Dad was helping Mom and me with the laundry, by running clothes through the wringer washing machine. Of course I wanted to help, too. When Dad turned his back, my arm went into the wringer of the machine and began the squeeze. When my arm was in the rollers almost to the elbow and I was crying out with pain, Dad—not knowing a latch would quickly release the wringer—reversed the process and my arm came rolling back out. No harm was done.

I was around four years old when I toppled off the second floor porch of the apartment, landing inches away from the sidewalk, which could have been a source of major trauma for me. A visit to our family friend, Doctor Shue, resulted in a cast to my forearm for some weeks.

Blairanne, about four

Mike was born when I was four years old and we still lived on Newberry Street. He was a 6lb-1oz baby. I am not aware of any problems with his birth, but he did not eat well and was very fragile. There were many visits to the doctor to monitor his apparent failure to thrive, He stayed a very thin child, but never to this day was there an understanding of the cause. Mom said her father, Grandpa Hamm, told her Mike would not live to one year.

Mike was diagnosed with scoliosis of the spine when a baby and had to wear therapeutic shoes until he was five or six. He also had special physical therapy as a child. And I think I remember that Mom stopped using the special shoes, as they were extremely expensive, and she decided he looked all right. He has never had any adverse problems from the uncertain condition he had as a child.

Many stories were told about me trying to get rid of him. I had been the center of attention for four years and felt invaded, I guess. The first "attempt" was not a genuine, deliberate act. I gave him a peanut to eat when he was barely one month old.

I sucked my thumb as a child, using a soft torn piece of sheet in my hand. On this occasion, I apparently crawled up on a chair and deposited my "blankie" on the bulb of a lamp, creating a smoke-filled living room and a four-month-old coughing baby. When Mom come inside after hanging wash out on the clothesline, she too was choking with smoke. Quick evacuation of the room averted a potential disaster for Mike. And again I was doing my thing, with no deliberation about my act, I am sure.

I don't remember emotional connections to those attempts to get rid of Mike, other than lifetime reminders of my acts. I wonder if Mike does. I will ask him.

My childhood was very safe, very stable and not laden with painful emotional experiences. In fact, I had this fallacious thought that I would deal well with the grief of losing my David because I had had little grief in my own life prior to this. I recognized, but only after 10 months of grieving, that I probably would have done better had I had to cope with painful trauma in my life. I was not prepared for the agony of losing my best friend and lover of 49 years, and I had to scramble to find ways to cope.

We moved to Bull Road when I was in first grade. Mom and Dad were able to purchase their own home, a small brick house with a basement, about two miles outside of town. It was 1949, and we did not have television. Dad rode to work with a co-worker at York Corporation for months before they acquired an auto. It was a 1936 Ford, which had the two back doors opening backwards.

One time I left the door open after exiting the car and Dad drove in the garage, stopping quickly, but only after some damage to the open door. That created an emotional response and crisis, but I don't remember it leaving an indelible mark.

We had three neighbor kids within 500 yards; Alan who was near Mike's age, and Barry who was near my age. Next door lived a family with a young disabled boy, but they largely ignored my family. However, when he was 10 and I was about 13 he taught me to play chess. He was an

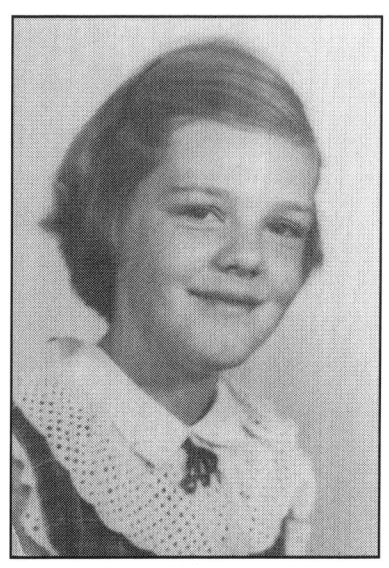
About seven years

excellent player. I never learned the game well enough to enjoy it—or to beat him.

A woman I called Aunt Helen lived with her brother down the road from us. He worked, but she never left the property. She cut her own hair, gardened, raised some rabbits and chickens, and lived a hermit existence, but she accepted me into her yard and house. She became for me a nurturing relationship, and she told me many stories about life. I was the only person mother knew of that she took into her house. I provided company for her.

We had a large garden in our back yard, and—as was customary at that time—Mom canned a lot of food for storage and our use during the winter. Every year I stuffed string beans into jars, always making certain they stood upright in the jar as Mom dictated. I picked strawberries and corn on the cob. Mike and I had our own roadside stand and sold fresh corn by the dozen, up to fifty cents a dozen one year. I helped peel tomatoes for sauce, peaches for canning, and I smashed apples for applesauce.

After dissecting the mouse, discovering it had babies in its abdomen, and being fascinated in this experience, I had announced to Dad I wanted to be a doctor. I then began my quest for that college experience. I was always trying to create a back-up plan for the field of Medicine, just in case. What if it doesn't work? What if I don't get accepted? What if there is no money?

I knew via many advisements that women were to marry, stay at home and raise the children of the marriage. There was no way I could accept that advice. Women in Medicine, the year I entered Medical School, was 7%, in contrast to the 52% of today. Physical therapy might provide for me an alternative choice to doctoring, but surely I would not be in charge and give the orders if I were only a Physical Therapist. I wanted to be in charge.

As I entered Junior High School it became apparent I was an achieving student and I continued my interest in Medicine. Dad let Mom go to work, acknowledging he had to prepare for my plans to continue my education. Mom's first job was cleaning houses. Then she became a waitress at the lunch counter in the Rea & Derick

Blairanne and Mike

Drug Store. Lunch was a busy time. Mom soon took over the management of the lunch counter and made it a profitable part of the store. She received bonuses and honors for her contribution to the store's success.

As a teen, I was in Girl Scouts and active in our church. Church was an important part of my family life. Wednesday night was family night, Sunday a.m. was church, and Sunday night there was always some activity. Luther League was a young people's meeting group.

In 9th grade at Central High School, students were clustered in sections according to their college potential. I was in 9-1 with the other excelling students. We were badgered and bullied as a group and soon began a close-knit relationship, enjoying many high-school activities together.

I was never singled out or chosen for dates, and remember vividly Mom's pride that I attended the Senior prom stag. I did have one romance with Karen's brother who was in college, but it was short-lived.

When a Lutheran retreat team visited our church, I fell madly in love with a member of that team. He even said he would return for my Prom but never responded to my communications after he left York.

I served on the Student Council for my high school and received some notoriety when our school hit the national press my senior year. Our school had a skirt length policy, and three girls arrived at school one day with skirts that were above the tips of the finger by the side length. They were promptly suspended. An already upset student body came to the attack with a sit-in in the school cafeteria, prompting more suspensions and many meetings with Administration and the press. I represented the student body in the discussions that followed the chaos. That was 1961. Our sit-in fit into a culture of young people who were becoming frustrated with life as it was defined by adults.

The sixties were upon us.

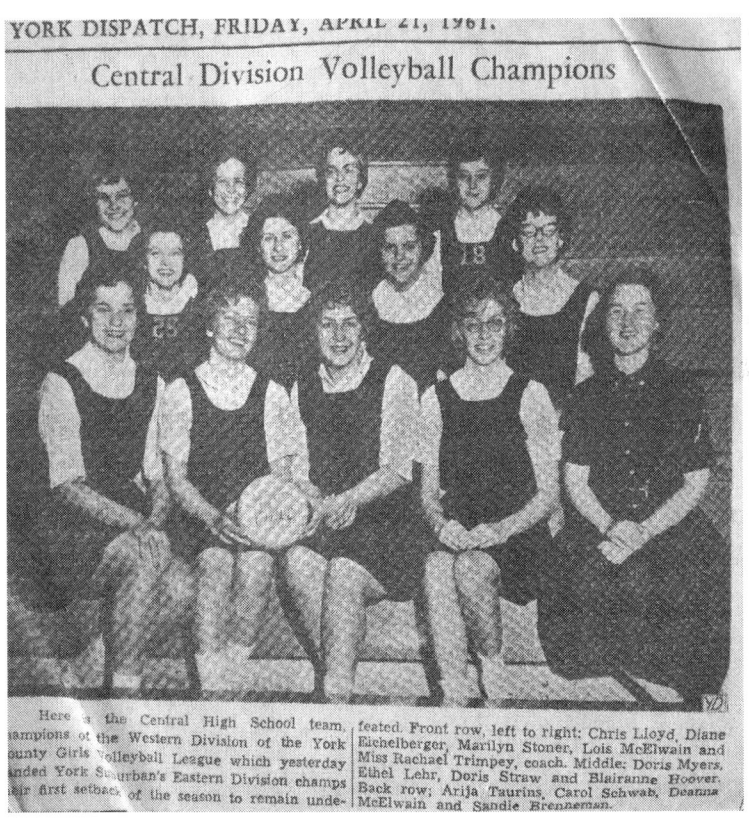

Blairanne, middle row, far right

BLAIRANNE HOOVER
R. D. No. 1

Academic   "B.H."

Serious thinker . . . understanding . . . says what she thinks . . . dependable worker . . . women's rights advocate and ardent Republican . . . Susquehanna bound . . .

Varsity Club, 3, 4 . . . F.T.A., 3, 4 . . . Chorus, 1, 2, 3, 4 . . . Business Manager, 4 . . . Field Hockey, 3, 4 . . . Volleyball, 2, 3, 4 . . . Student Council, 4 . . . Y-Teens, 1 . . . Prowler Staff, 2, 3, 4.

I had wanted to attend Bucknell University, as I'd heard it was a good Pre-Med school. But Dad insisted on Susquehanna University. The family physician, Doctor Shue, along with our Pastor, Pastor Moorhead, and our Ophthalmologist, were all alumni. Dad saw some help there for the possibility of financial aid for my education. I did receive work grants and some scholarship money.

My work grant made me an assistant to the dormitory house mother. That is an obsolete function these days on college campuses, but it was important in those days. My freshman year, the house mother waited at the door as we slipped in at the sound of chimes at 8 p.m. weekday nights. We were allowed to extend to two 10 p.m. curfews when we had the need. And Saturday night we were allowed a midnight curfew. I was responsible for the monitoring of student compliance to these and other house rules. In my senior year, the house mother did not show up and I was shifted to acting house mother. A lot of extra work followed that promotion. And to top it off, there was an epidemic of German measles on campus. I had the opportunity to monitor and care for multiple students in bed with an acute illness. I was already seeing my medical career in its infancy. It is interesting, as the vaccine for German measles became widely available in 1963. And the testing for German Measles immunity was available when I was pregnant with Heather, and I was already immune. I could have guessed that after my caregiving job as a college student.

During my junior and senior years I was on the Student Government Board and Vice President for Women my senior year. We were largely responsible for disciplining errant students, including those who broke campus rules like visiting the Governor Snyder Hotel bar, which was off limits. It made for an interesting dynamic, as I was now interested in, and during that year began dating, David.

David not only lived at the Governor Snyder Hotel, but cleaned the restrooms at the bar and occasionally served as bartender. Questions were asked, but as far as the administration knew, I never frequented the place.

While I was a sophomore at Susquehanna, Dad was offered a position with his company, Borg Warner, at the Food Fair warehouse in Philadelphia. Though he was not an engineer he was intimately associated with the development of the system of heat and cooling used for food storage. Mom, Dad and Mike moved to Woodbury, New Jersey. Dad spent many years maintaining the system, and was forced to retire when he fell from a ladder, breaking both of his heels.

Mike graduated from high school in Woodbury and attended Susquehanna, entering after my graduation. He was active in Theta Chi Fraternity, and majored in Psychology. During an Internship at a hospital in western Pennsylvania he met nurse Peg Wareham. They married, and when Mike entered the army they lived with Mom and Dad in Woodbury. He was stationed at Fort Dix, near the house. They started their family with Tracy and later added Michelle. After he was out of the service they moved to Greeley, Colorado, where Mike obtained his D,Ed. He then served many years at the helm of the school districts as a school psychologist and was active in developing many programs, including residential student programs at the district and debriefing programs for student traumatic events.

Peg worked as a school nurse, heading up the department and, along with Mike, teaching at the University of Northern Colorado. They have two grandchildren living in Fort Collins with Tracy and Brian, and three grandchildren in Portland Oregon with Michelle and Mitch.

While we were child-raising and busy with work we saw little of each other. Weddings and graduations brought us together. Mike and David shared crazy humor and were always in a jousting of humorous compliments. As retirement approached we spent more time in visits.

And as David became very ill, Mike, and especially Peg, became very intimate in their support of our family. The last days and hours of David's life were enriched by their presence and support. One could never ask for more in the presence and availability of a grief partner than I've had in Peg over the years since David's death.

Speaking of David. I had not dated and was pretty much a loner as a college student. I was always able to justify this role, as I wanted to study hard to go to Medical School, and I was always on call for the dormitory, so I had a lot of responsibility.

But I did see this football player in the snack bar often. I heard that he wrote poetry and I heard he liked the opera and that he was living off campus at the Governor Snyder Hotel. He was certainly an atypical Susquehanna student. And then I discovered him in my microbiology class. He came to the 8 a.m. class dressed in the work fatigues required at the Selinsgrove State School, and he often fell asleep during class. To top it off, he would get a higher grade on exams than I did. In those days grades were posted near the classroom door by name. I knew I had to meet this guy. It was in histology class that we officially met, and that experience set the future of our relationship.

John & Annabelle Hoover

Blairanne with brother Mike and their Dad

*Standing: Christian, Alea, Jesse, Peg, Blair,
Seated: Mike and Amaya - 2013*

Chapter 6
We Meet

DAVID …

Students were paired up for lab, and there was some conflict in our schedules where neither Blair or I could take lab with the rest of the class, so we were matched up. Now, working more closely together, I saw her differently; especially after the frog incident. We were studying the effects of spinal cord destruction known as pithing a frog. As Blair inserted the pointed tool into the spinal cord of her frog, it made a croaking sound causing her to jump and drop the frog. As I retrieved her frog from the floor I saw a different, more fragile side of her, and realized that what I had thought was aloofness, was just shyness. Now, I took an immediate liking to her. She smelled good and looked good, and was just delightful to be with.

We began dating, and I already knew I wanted to marry her, but she told me she was going to marry a doctor. Not one to be deterred, I began taking pre-med classes. We studied together, taking all the "ologies." I earned many "A"s in science and planned to take botany or zoology in graduate school and ultimately teach at the college level. Blair was accepted into medical school, and I was accepted at Duke and Rutgers, We talked more about marriage, but Blair didn't want to marry if we would be living apart—and she wanted me to go to medical school.

We both graduated from Susquehanna in the spring of 1965, and Blair went off to the Woman's Medical School in Philadelphia, where she was elected class president her junior year. I was continuing on for another year at Susquehanna, taking the additional courses needed to get a chemistry major and get into medical school. I was required to take 12 to 15 credits to keep from going to Vietnam. Luckily, I thought college was fun. Maybe that's why I spent over six years as an undergraduate.

We continued seeing each other when we could. I lived with a group of guys that fall semester, which was a huge mistake. They partied all the time and ate all my sandwiches, and the noise was just too much, so I left there during the Christmas break.

Blair and I became engaged that Christmas of 1965. Her father said, "You never asked me for her hand. How will you be able to afford marriage and both of you going to medical school at the same time?"

I pointed out that we only needed one set of medical books. I always saw the positive side of things. I had always been frugal, and wasn't too concerned about how we would afford marriage. And I was going to auctions on weekends and buying furniture for us.

We had to attend pre-marriage counseling, and Blair's pastor, Pastor Snyder, was reluctant to give us communion during the wedding. He evidently didn't think I was religious enough. I said, "At least I'm telling you the truth, not what you want to hear. Probably 90% of the people who come in here tell you what you want to hear, and then go out and do the opposite."

He finally agreed to marry us, but stopped short of giving us communion. It wasn't that I didn't have faith, I just didn't buy into the structured religion. I was going to church and singing in a choir while in college, because I believed you met more nice people in church than you would meet in a bar. Five years later, after finishing med school, I was teaching Sunday school at the church we were married in, and we became good friends with the pastor who had performed our ceremony.

That year finally ended; I graduated and received my acceptance to medical school; and Blair and I were ready to begin life together. After learning we couldn't get married in the new Mt. Zion church because it hadn't been dedicated yet, plans had to be adjusted to be married in the old church. As it happened we are in the history books for being the last couple married in the old Mt. Zion Church. We were married on Saturday, June 18, 1966. Blair's father had said there would be no booze at the wedding, but we (or should I say, I) disregarded that, and he imbibed as much as anyone. After the reception, which had been held at the local fire hall, we were so tired we drove three miles down the road and stayed at the Playland Motel. The next day, Sunday, we drove back to Selinsgrove and I was back at work that night.

Wedding day - June 18, 1966

I had planned to quit working at Selinsgrove State School in 1965, but Blair and I were spending our first married summer there. Blair was doing research on Downs Syndrome. I was working nights, Thursday through Sunday, and Blair was working 8:00 a.m. to 5:00 p.m., Monday through Friday, so we weren't seeing a lot of each other during that period.

While working nights I'd go to the other wards, and was free to get all the data needed for our research, which Blair would work on during the day. We published a paper on our findings and received some grant money for it.

Several years later, the state stopped the farm work at the school, having decided that using the kids to work was "slave labor." I believed that was the worst thing they could have done. The kids needed something to do. Without good, healthy, outdoor work, they just sat around smoking and getting fat. The school wouldn't give them cigarettes, but they could have pipes or pouch tobacco to chew on.

Along with ending the work program, the hospital released many people who should not have been let out—people with major mental problems. Those individuals were more likely to commit a crime, walk in front of a train, or become a victim to violence while on the street. It was—in my opinion—a stupid thing to do.

That summer we lived in a farmhouse owned by a professor we had become friends with. We would also house-sit, or pet-sit when friends were gone. We did a lot of antiquing, and picked up old furniture at auctions or yard sales. I was buying so much at auctions that some thought I was an antique dealer. I refinished the furniture, and we kept some pieces and sold others.

I kept that interest in antiques all our lives. In fact, I'll share a story about when we were students in medical school in Philadelphia. I was looking through a trash heap on a sidewalk one day, and had just picked up a butter churn, when an older woman stuck her head outside the door.

"What are you doing with that?" she asked.

"I thought you were throwing it away. I was going to fix it up," I said. "I'm a medical student, and learned to love antiques."

She invited me in, offered me coffee, and we talked a while. As I was leaving, she pointed to a nicer butter churn near the door and said, "Take this one, it's in better shape than the one in the trash."

When I protested, she said, "My kids won't want it, and will probably just toss it out when I'm gone. Take it."

So I did, but, never one to miss an opportunity, I asked, "Can I still take the one from the trash, too?"

I loved making old things look new again, and at the time it provided extra income. I enjoy it just as much today, as a hobby.

Besides refinishing furniture and antiques, I was always looking for ways to earn and save money. I would buy old clunker cars that were several years old, and fix them up.

My first car was a 1949 Chrysler that I only paid a couple of hundred bucks for. Over the next several years I owned three '59 Chevys that I paid about $50 each for. One got hit by a bus, and another died on the expressway. I took all my stuff out of it, took the license plate off and walked home, abandoning it where it was.

One of the Chevys came with four snow tires and a lot of rust. I put layers of masking tape over the rust spot and sprayed it with gray paint for the inspection. Of course it didn't fool anyone. The inspector looked at it and said, "You gotta be kidding me!" Then he took pity on me and relented, saying, "Okay, I'll let it go this time, but don't bring it back that way again."

While I was at Susquehanna, I had a Nash Rambler with no muffler. I cut both ends out of tin cans and wired them together to form a makeshift muffler. A friend saw this contraption and offered to put a real muffler on for me. The battery was usually dead on this car, so I had to park on a hill and release the emergency brake to give it a rolling start.

When the summer of '66 ended, we moved to Philadelphia. I was beginning my freshman year in med school at the Philadelphia College of Osteopathy, and Blair was starting her second year at the the Woman's Medical College. It wasn't easy, but we hadn't expected it to be. I felt like I was finally my own man. I wanted to do well in this, and said to myself, "If they tell me to shit green, I will. I will dress appropriately and never miss a class. I will do everything by the rules."

I had a decent living, a wonderful wife, and I was going to be a doctor.

We moved into the Abbottsford public housing in Philadelphia—a mostly black project that only cost us $50 a month. As a married couple, we could get some benefits that singles didn't get. Abbottsford wasn't the greatest place to live, but it was cheap, and close to the Woman's Medical School, so Blair could walk to school. We were robbed once while we lived there, and there were often fights in the housing area. We held our stethoscopes up against the wall to listen to the loud arguments next door. One guy threw his wife out the window. When I tried to go to her aid the guy threatened me, using some very colorful language. I took his threats seriously, backed off, and called the cops. The housing was only a mile from where the Temple riots took place after Martin Luther King was assassinated in 1968.

The College of Osteopathy was interesting, and I was enjoying it. There were two years of school work and by the third year we were spending time with patients. We were required to wear a coat and tie every day so that we would look like professionals, unlike today when doctors can get away with looking scruffy. The theory was, if we looked like a doctor, we would think like a doctor.

As a fourth year med student, I made the rounds with doctors, was involved in the care of patients, took notes, and learned from the process. One day while a group of med students was making rounds, an elderly patient was staring at me. She said, "Young man come in here!"

I went into her room, and she said, "You have the highest blue around you that I've ever seen."

I didn't know what she meant at the time, but she explained it to me. She said, "I see auras of different colors around people. Blue is a healing light, and you have a great deal of blue around you. I've noticed that when you see a patient, you talk to them and put your hand on them, and I can see that blue light going from you into the patient."

She said I would be an excellent physician because of this light and empathy. I began visiting her every day after rounds and she told me more about it. She said, "When I was young I told my parents about the colors, but they didn't know what I was talking about. I thought everybody saw them, and was surprised to learn that they don't."

I asked her about another doctor, who everybody thought was a jerk, to put it kindly. He had no rapport at all with patients, and no one liked him, including the students and other doctors. She said, "When he goes into a room, he actually sucks the blue out of a patient when he sees them."

She also mentioned a popular radiologist, saying he was in the wrong field, because he had a huge blue aura about him. "He touches you, and you just feel better when he's around," she said.

In the summer of 1968, we got out of the city for a while to do an externship in the hills of Appalachia in West Virginia. It was a different world for us. Some of these people hadn't seen a doctor in years. We learned many valuable lessons about practicing primary care medicine.

Blair got pregnant that summer, which wasn't the best timing, as she was pregnant during her entire senior year of medical school, and gave birth to Heather during finals. She wanted to become pregnant then as she knew the next internship year would be too stressful to be pregnant. She persevered, accomplishing it all like a trooper, and graduated from medical school the spring of 1969.

Blair interned at Germantown hospital in Philadelphia, and I continued with my final year at Philadelphia College of Osteopathy. I became primary care giver for Heather that year as Blair worked a heavy schedule with every third night on call at the hospital.

I was enjoying Osteopathy, because there was a lot more to the healing. It involves psychiatry, manipulation, talking and listening for better understanding … and a lot of touching. These days so much is done with ultrasounds, CT scans, and other machinery, that no one is touching anymore. But healing comes with touching and empathy.

I was still working a lot that last year. On Friday nights I would leave medical school and go to my second job at the Metropolitan Hospital where I worked all night until 5:00 a.m. A buddy had trained me to be a lab technician, and I would take blood from donors. I was also doing research, injecting mice with a clam extract: Venus mercenaria that was being studied to treat a cancer. The mice were injected with the extract, kept happy, and after they died, I would cut the tumor out. Part of my job was to order the mice, but I soon realized I could breed them myself. Mice would have a new litter about every 19 days, with six to eight babies per litter, so it was easy to produce all we needed. The benefit of doing this was that I could keep the money the school would have paid for them. I was always thinking!

My years of hard work and study finally paid off, and I graduated from medical school in June of 1970. I served my internship at York Memorial Osteopathic Hospital, where I delivered over 100 babies. I didn't always feel prepared to do so, but there were many times when I was the only doctor available on short notice. The rule of see one, do one, teach one even disappeared sometimes as I just had to do. I learned a lot of medicine that year. Blair had completed her internship and was working as the physician in a nursing home.

By the time I graduated, I had been in college almost continuously since 1958, and had majored in business, chemistry and medicine. I loved being in classrooms and I loved learning. I'm glad I became a doctor, but I think I would have been successful in any field, because I was always interested in learning about new things; everything from antiques to zoology.

Chapter 7
Heather

He taught us that "Repetition is the mother of learning."
Proof: We all can repeat all his lectures to us verbatim.

BLAIR ...

The boys did not have special privilege to that admonition. More than once Heather found herself in the hands of the father, who admonished and elaborated on the importance of good choices and good behavior. And the story often repeated itself as the kids repeated some unacceptable behaviors in the venture to do their teen years. And so, as Dad repeated the admonishing they all said they knew his words of good behavior and his words of making good choices. Incidentally, "good choices" was the common out-the-door, goodbye, have fun, directive they heard. So when the parental lecture started and they protested having heard it many times before, David would reply "repetition is the mother of learning."

The clinching honor came to David when Heather, the teacher, came into the house laughing and shaking her head in self-disclosure. "Dad, I can't believe it, guess what I told my 9th grade science class today when they whined at my discipline. You need to hear this. Remember 'Repetition is the mother of learning?' I never thought I'd be quoting my Dad, and here I am; just as you said."

Heather was our first child. I had planned to have her before doing my Internship, as I was getting older and would not be able to have her during that time of having every third night on call and long days and minimal sleep. I was awarded a scholarship to do rural medicine as a Junior student. Together, we spent a summer in Wise, West Virginia where I worked with a family doc, and David assisted at the local miner's hospital. It was there we started our family. So Heather was delivered my Senior year while I was on Psychiatry rotation. The Dean, having heard I was pregnant, called and offered me a schedule change so I would be finished with my Surgery rotation before her birth. I took the National Board Exam ten days after her birth, seated on pillows and pumping breasts during the break. And just to show how hard I studied, I obtained honors in Obstetrics and Gynecology on that exam.

The next year I was Interning at Germantown Hospital while David was a senior student. He handled a lot of Heather's care, as I was at the hospital many hours. It was when she was seven months old and crying in the middle of my sleep with no consolation, that I retracted my wish for 12 children and told David six should be enough for us to handle.

As soon as Heather was barely 13 months old, we adopted Matthew as a newborn infant, and her life was disrupted.

We quickly set up practice in Bloomsburg PA after being recruited there. We found a home just across the Susquehanna River from town and the hospital. Heather was wrangled into child care at two-and-a-half, though they were only accepting three-year-olds. And we began the long journey of seeking and finding childcare people. We nearly always had people living with us in our basement, which had a hot plate and a bathroom. College students were frequently in need of a place to stay, and were hosted with a commitment to be available for child care, especially when both David and I needed to be out of the house. Leszak came to the university as a Polish immigrant to wrestle and we were called, as people thought David might speak Polish. Over the months we learned a lot of Polish as Leszak and Maria became extended family. We even hosted their wedding, with Matthew and Heather wearing Polish costumes. They later moved to their own quarters with the birth of their daughter. Leszak became an engineer and we continue to keep in touch to this day.

Our kids were constantly on stage and—for much of their lives—living in a small community with parents who were well-known and highly visible, resulting in having many standards to honor. Matthew shocked me with the story that he and Charles never paid to go to the movies. They always got the recognition from the sales person at the theater and were told, "Go ahead, your dad is my doctor; he is so wonderful." And Shally reports that parental connection saved her on traffic tickets on at least one occasion when the police officer who stopped her for speeding told her he'd let her go. "Tell your Dad I said Hi," was her directive. Heather, much later in her adolescent years, told of the party that was raided by the police and she exited quickly through a window in the house. While many friends got in deep trouble, she walked away, innocent.

Speaking of sneaking teens, Heather was caught in more than one of those occasions. A sneak trip to visit a friend in western PA resulted in our knowledge when a patient reported seeing her 250 miles from home. He didn't know that a sleepover at a friends' house was without the parents' knowledge.

The kids learned many lessons when we ventured to the Navajo Reservation. Heather was 12 years old, Anglo —as we were known politely by the Navajo (Belligana in a disparaging way)—and one of seven Anglo kids in the 250-student high school. She suffered at the hands of many Navajo kids. Name calling and shoving were not uncommon and she quickly reported she understood why her friend, the first black girl in her class back in PA, had cried a lot. Every day she came home crying. I gave my well-learned Christian admonition to "turn the other cheek," while David gave directives to "beat the girl up." After four weeks of turning, she beat the girl up. Though she thought we would be called by the principal for disciplinary action, it never occurred. The upside of switching from "turn the other cheek" to "beat her up" was that the harassment stopped. And Heather later joined the H.S. girls' basketball team and traveled with the team on long trips. No problems occurred again.

It was on the Navajo reservation that Heather met and fell in love with Adam at age 11. His mother, Gennie, was a nurse who joined our team at Crownpoint soon after David and I started on the medical staff. She had moved to the Indian Health Service after frustration working as a detective with the police system in their home town of Key West Florida.

Adam and Matthew became good friends as a team of young boys exploring the high desert of New Mexico, catching lizards and shooting BB guns at moving varmints, as well as riding horses through dense cacti. Adam and Heather fell in love. And after a year, when Gennie said it was time to move on to Oklahoma to another HIS facility, they both mourned and cried the loss of their young romance. Minimal contact through a few letters left us believing that she had "gotten over it" as we had predicted. When Heather was graduating from high school, Gennie called and invited Heather to come to Key West and participate, as she was still very much in Adam's mind. He had been working for the police department as a dispatcher and had plans to stay on there. He obtained his degree in vocational technology.

Heather returned home dedicated to her renewed love for Adam and a plan to return to him. A year of college preparatory at Perkioman school caught her up in her studies. It was apparent after our return from the Reservation that her good acclimatization to the life there included her failure to progress in high school studies, and that the grades at Central's graduation were not going to move her into college.

We had recognized significant losses for her and Matthew when we returned from the Reservation, but the High School refused to hold them back, saying they would catch up. And that did not happen for either of them at Central. Matthew moved on to a private school setting and Heather advanced at a preparatory school. One year after a junior college stint at Keystone Junior College, and a winter working near school on the snow patrol, Heather reported that life could only be lived happily if she moved to be with Adam in Key West. His mother agreed and approved, and that was Heather's move to the big world.

After one semester at the community college with Adam in classes with her, they decided to move to New Mexico to go to college together at New Mexico State University in Las Cruces. Adam had one visit to our home in Pennsylvania. It was Christmas and snowy, and as he sat by the fireplace with his coat on, he announced that he would never live further north than the line created by Interstate 10. That pretty much limited them to the metropolitan areas of Miami, Dallas, El Paso, Phoenix, and San Diego.

While attending NMSU, Adam excelled as a Crimson Scholar, graduating with honors. Heather did well in Education, even beating him in one history class they took together. Heather admitted that Adam was the excelling editor of her home assignments and papers. Heather played on an adult soccer team while at NMSU, and while playing in a soccer tournament in Phoenix, they decided together that was the part of the country they would like to call home. While in college, married status would improve their living opportunities, and one Friday, July 13th, they visited the JP and declared their vows. Twenty-five years later, and this week as I am writing, they continue their great love and respect for each other and are celebrating with a weekend in Las Vegas.

The products of their love, Alea and Christian, complete an intimate family of love and shared family travels and ventures. Alea is the shy, quiet, excelling honors Sophomore student at ASU, living at home after a Freshman year on campus. She is in the W.P. Carey school of honors in business and works part time at the "Chop Shop" serving healthy food including smoothies.

Christian is swimming regularly with instruction and team participation at Chandler High School and spends great numbers of hours playing video games.

Heather taught junior high for fourteen years and is now enjoying high-school students, especially guiding the honors students in their ventures in life. Adam started his work, after earning a criminal justice degree, in the probation system in the Phoenix, Glendale and Gilbert Courts. He now is the Head Court Administrator for Gilbert and is being wooed by other metropolitan areas to make a move. He is strongly committed to the town of Gilbert and its future and to the stability for his family of living in Gilbert.

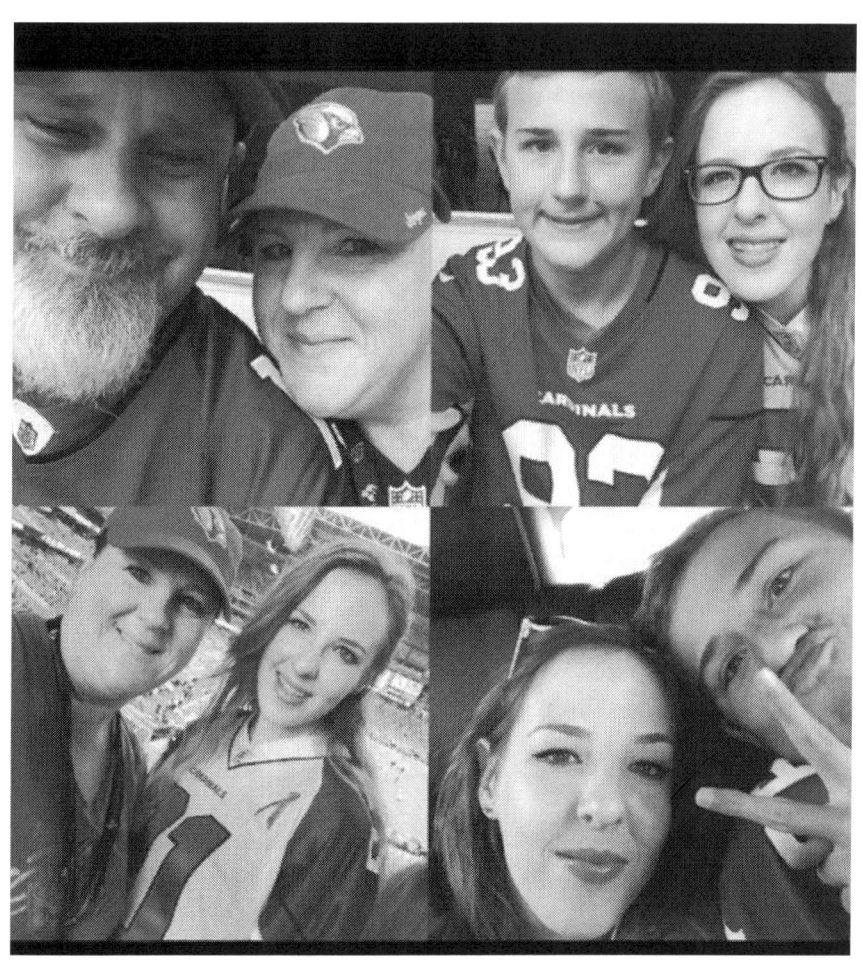

Clockwise from left:
Adam & Heather, Christian & Alea
Heather & Alea, Alea & Christian

Chapter 8
Began Internship

DAVID ...

When I began my internship in York in 1970, we had moved into our first real home; a three-bedroom rental. Blair and I were both working in careers we loved, we had our little daughter Heather and our own place. Life was good.

In January of 1971, we had an opportunity to adopt a child. Blair had always admired Roy Rogers and Dale Evans for adopting so many kids, and used to say she wanted to have twelve of her own, and adopt twelve more. After Heather was born, Blair revised that number to a total of six.

Both of us regularly referred families and unwed pregnant girls to an adoption agency, Tressler Lutheran Social Services, and Blair struck up a connection with one of the women who worked there. When we seriously began looking into adoption, we were told it would be a two-year process. We began the process with group meetings with other adoptive parents. Two months after our application a baby boy was born in Texas; did we want to take him, they said. Yes, it will be awhile until your approval, then travel must be arranged, so you have time. The next week we received a call saying our baby would arrive the following week!

Chapter 9
Matthew

"I'm going to lose 20 pounds by Christmas."

BLAIR ...
Charles listed this high on his list of Dad's quotations. A diet was the usual routine for David, on and off, over and over again. When we married in June of 1966, he was pretty trim, though he complained of being overweight. A few bites shared with you about food, that really defined a lot of our relationship, cannot be missed.

Food, and the family focus on the preparation, serving and eating of food, varies from one household to the next, no matter what the cultural heritage. It is true that heritage does make its way onto the family table. And I chose Matthew under this quote of David's as Matthew moved on to become a specialist in food and food preparation.

My first visit to David's home and the kitchen table provided much learning about a culture and about my potential future in-laws. My mother-in-law, Anna, stood as she served the dinners and rarely sat at the table while the family—David, Pop, and I—ate. She was ready to refill the bowl of beans, add extra hot gravy from the kettle and pour the cup of coffee Pop ordered when he had eaten, clearing his plate of every bite of food.

I assumed this was the Russian/Slovak way of family feeding. I was more enlightened when, at lunch, sandwiches were prepared as we ate. Anna stood at the end of the table and lathered the freshly cut bread with mayonnaise. Then she applied the various ingredients to our order as we sat at the table.

On occasion when the conversation slipped into the realm of "don't let the company and kids know our issues," the language shifted to Russian, Slovak and/or a mixture of both. David was always instructed to speak English, with the admonition, "you are an American." We wondered how they might have communicated if he knew what was being said.

My future with David was predicted and decided by Anna after my first visit to David's home. It was her homemade lasagna, which required three days' notice to prepare for us. It was special, as it was my first visit to Mt Carmel. That evening Anna told David her observation of our relationship. I was off to bed and they were sharing mother-son moments while Pop made his rounds of the bars. "You will marry this girl," he quoted to me later that week. "Mom declared that to me immediately after you went to bed."

And he followed her statement with his own question, "How do you know I will marry this girl?"

"This is the first girl you brought home that I saw you eat off her plate," she said. "I know you are going to marry her."

Yes, she was right, and that habit became a typical function of food in our relationship. Commonly, David would reach across for that extra bite, taking from my plate. I later told him that was how he got fat. I stayed thin, he grew as he ate off my plate.

He was also known to do that to his kids. For some reason it was most pronounced when he did it to Matthew. Matthew would form a tent around his plate with his arms, always upset that Dad wanted to invade his dinner.

While David was interning in York, I joined a group, then popularly known as a Transcendental Meditation group. One of the women in the group was the Executive Director of Tressler Lutheran Social Services adoption agency. A perfect time to begin our adoptive family. That goal of 6 adopted and 6 biological children was always in my mind. Of course the change to 3 and 3 was easy when Heather was at that 7 month age. I always admired Roy Rogers and Dale Evans who had 24 adopted children on their ranch. So many children need homes. And a funny memory I always had of passing an orphanage in York as a child seemed to have been an indelible marker for me for adoption. I remember clearly, brother Mike asking dad if he would die soon, so he could go to that orphanage, as they had a horse we always saw in the yard.

Heather was barely 15 months old but we were advised that until we did the paper work and got approval it would be probably two years.

In fact, it would be less than a week before we received the call, and another week before we received the baby! He was 10 days old. All we knew was that his mother and father were in the Army. His dad was Puerto Rican and mother was of Mexican heritage, Aztec we were told.

David was on call, so some friends went with me to Baltimore airport, where the baby would arrive from Brooke Army Medical Center in San Antonio. I had never flown before, and thought it ironic that our nearly newborn son would arrive on a plane. The flight was delayed five hours, and I could hardly stand the waiting, I was so excited. It was a most exciting time. The airline hostesses helped the social worker who brought two babies to Pennsylvania. He had been in foster care for four days before flying to us.

The baby had black hair that stood straight up, and when we first saw him we thought he smelled funny, but the scent disappeared after a while. He cried a lot at first, but overall, was a happy baby. We named our new son Matthew David. Our little family was growing.

Matthew's black, stand-on-end hair was never a comb-flat hair. His heritage was questioned by many kind observers in Pennsylvania: "Is he Japanese?" they'd ask. And when confronted by curious observers I would, in David's absence, say, "he looks just like his father."

When Matthew was nine months old Grandpa Revak was cuddling him on his lap when he began talking about our move from the city-center of Philadelphia to rural Bloomsburg. "Aren't you glad to be up here away from all the blacks and Puerto Ricans?" he questioned.

"Pop," David smiled, "Matthew is Mexican and Puerto Rican."

One of the stories that demonstrated the transparency of David and me in the community as physicians has to do with Matthew. He never slept longer than four hours until he was 10 months old. David would hold and cuddle him until late at night. Once he was in his crib I would put a bag of cheerios and a Tommy Tippee cup filled with ice and orange juice, hoping he wouldn't call until 6 a.m. A mother struggling with a baby who wouldn't sleep told me she knew of the orange juice and the cheerios I used for Matthew. It was true that if patients didn't observe or hear stories about us, David was certain to fill them in with his stories.

Matthew proved to us that adoption is a wonderful experience. Our previous experience with adoption was mostly related to folks who had fertility issues. People questioned that when we spoke of adoption. No, we just want to give kids a home; it was simple. And when we adopted Matthew we had little information about his heritage. Would his biologic mother come looking for him? I wondered. Could we handle that experience?

One day when Matthew was about two years old I was interviewing a new patient who had just left the military with her husband in Texas. She was pregnant. In taking her history she confessed that she had had a baby two years earlier and gave it up for adoption. What? I thought to myself. She was Hispanic, she gave her baby for adoption and she was in the military with her husband in Texas. Could this be Matthew's biologic mother? I was shaking as I led the conversation to more detail including the date of delivery; no, it was not Matthew's mother. Thank God, I thought, he is my son forever.

Later, when we spent two years on an Indian reservation, we thought that would be a good venture for Matthew, since he is of Puerto Rican and Mexican heritage. His dark skin—which got darker in the high sun—and his black, straight, cow-lick hair, were going to fit the look of the Navajo boys. He started fifth grade at the reservation elementary school, which had a population of about 60 students. Matthew was one of five non-Navajo kids attending, and he was harassed and bullied. They knew he didn't belong. How naïve of us!

Having pencil points stuck into the palm of his hand was one way he rose to the acknowledgement of "not belonging here." He soon met and befriended a very blonde boy, Adam, who would become a life-long friend and future brother-in-law. They had many days riding horses and playing cowboys with a BB gun Adam had brought with him from Key West. The boys had many great times together.

Our family always shared meals together at the table. With five children—four of them teenagers—meals were somewhat frantic. Back on the reservation, when we'd had just three children and pretty consistent 8-5 work hours, meals seemed manageable. We lived in a government block house on the Reservation, right by the hospital, and the on-call schedule was not usually too burdensome. We had wonderful times together and food was always a home deal.

There was a Kentucky Fried Chicken in Crownpoint, but our closest hamburger place was 50 miles away in Gallup, New Mexico. On rare occasions we needed to get away from the clinic and our home, and a trip to Gallup was our venture. We were usually on-call two out of six weekends, and we travelled whenever we both had a weekend free.

Seriously ill or injured patients often required one of us to bounce in the back of an ambulance to Gallup. On one occasion David sent a medical student on the plane flying a patient to Albuquerque through a snow storm. The pilot said he could manage the directions by following Interstate 40, as the snow created a white-out of the land.

When we first arrived on the reservation we had our Pace Arrow motor home. David had it packed so that when clinic closed at 5 p.m. on Friday we were ready to hit the road. We often went to Albuquerque in the motor home, but sometimes we'd drive the car and stay in the Marriott, which had a pool and a game room. On Sunday, before traveling the 120 miles back to Crownpoint, we'd buy our supply of groceries.

After a few short months of using the RV in the state and National Parks campgrounds, the kids voted for the real camping venture and insisted on tents and sleeping bags. The first weekend of tenting we went to Elephant Butte State Park. The wind had decided to swirl through the lakeside as we arrived and our attempts at setting up a tent became ventures of David yelling and trying to recruit help, while the kids were busy finding rocks and other collectibles on the beach.

With practice, we all became good at setting up camp and soon enjoyed cooking over a Coleman stove or a fire pit, and keeping warm amidst strange sounds of nature and the chill of a snowy Colorado high-elevation site. We enjoyed the camping life and returned to Pennsylvania thinking we could continue that joy.

Our first venture in PA was to Ricketts Glen State Park. And our first night turned into disaster when, unknown to us, the flow of heavy rain water through the park found its way through our tent. We decided we didn't have the skills to camp "back East" and quickly dispensed with the gear.

On our second Thanksgiving on the reservation, Matthew and David joined Gary and Mark Briley for a one-week, 20-plus mile hike into and out of the Grand Canyon. David and Gary trained for months before the trip, carrying gallons of water on their backs. Matthew should have done more conditioning with his Dad, as he pooped out about halfway out of the canyon and required some aid with his supplies. But a week of hiking and living the primitive life was a wonderful memory for him.

Cowboy Bill was the lover of one of our nurses who came to Crownpoint shortly after our arrival. When we discovered the kids were well beyond boredom in the isolated area of Navajo high desert, while Mom and Dad were hard at work, we appealed to Bill for horseback riding lessons for the kids. Of course that resulted in a need for horses and we began a venture of horse trading that carried us through ownership of more than seven horses and at least five birth events; the last occurring after we brought four horses back to Pennsylvania at the end of our two-year stint on the Navajo Reservation.

Matthew carried much of those experiences with him for over a year. To get the horses from the canyon, and often for ease of riding, the kids rode bareback. Matthew usually was aback Shamu, who, in her unpredictable, unsettled way, would stop abruptly to see how the rider was doing or to simply buck the load off her back. On two occasions Matthew found himself addressing a cactus plant and hundreds of imbedded needles. For more than a year we were plucking festering cactus needles out with tweezers.

After two years on the reservation we were going to be moving to Oklahoma to a small community where the kids could attend public schools and the Indian hospital was in the town by the public hospital. David by this time had had it with the government system, not being willing to comply with the strict system and the "politics " of the hospitals. So we returned to Bloomsburg. The kids returned to old friends and our summers were rich with time spent by Fishing Creek in a cottage we bought to live in while we sought a permanent residence. Friends had cottages and visited. The telephone company installed a box on a tree at first so David could take calls from the creek. Later we had phone service in the cottage. The kids fished, tubed the creek rapids after hard rains and enjoyed times with each other and friends.

It was here Matthew was clearly identified as a food man, though we did not see it in the career form till later. He loved catching crayfish and cooking and eating them himself. Always when we ate out he ordered the finest entrée on the menu, often a steak or shrimp special.

When we returned from the two years on the Navajo Reservation, the three kids were significantly behind their grade level of accomplishment. Early testing put Heather below the level of reading she had reached when we left for the reservation during her 7th grade year. Shally was young enough in 1st grade that we weren't worried. We suspected that Matthew had also lost ground.

I spoke to the principal at Central when we returned to Pennsylvania asking that Matthew and Heather be held back a grade. He argued with me, saying, "they will be fine."

I always honored the educator opinion. But it wasn't long before we realized we were correct. We regretted not doing more intervention with their education on the reservation, and now they were destined to make major changes to catch them up.

Our surgeon friend had sent his son to a Catholic boys' school in Spring Grove, three hours from Bloomsburg, to help him advance. We decided that would be a good plan for Matthew. The school closed in his second year and we never knew how much it helped him academically. He did share that it was there he learned to drink alcohol.

We brought him back to Bloomsburg and enrolled him in another private school within driving distance of home. By then he was really not interested in academics, but was caught up enough to stay on track and finally come home and graduate from Bloomsburg High School. The next venture was to Penn Tech Junior college

The boys played soccer while in school. Matthew played soccer for Bloomsburg High School after an attempt at the private school, Wyoming Seminary. Before the season began he had an eye injury when hit by a ball. The ophthalmologist told him no soccer for the season. The next year when he attended Bloomsburg High School, his excellent soccer skills helped the team win the county championship.

But someone went to the PIAA protesting, saying Matthew had been an illegal player. We had specifically advised Coach Wolfe about the eye incident at Wyoming, and he said it was taken care of: it wasn't. The team lost the championship because of Matthew's ineligibility.

By this time Matthew had been reaching beyond the confines of legal drinking and was covering his stress in an unhealthy manner. During the year at Penn Tech, where he started in culinary arts, he had a major accident, losing control of a car while under the influence of alcohol. He hit a large sign along the highway. A courtesy call from the police, with his admission of the alcohol problem, helped him move on to a rehabilitation center. He spent one month at Chit Chat Farms near Reading PA; an experience that was life-saving.

While there for a family meeting, parents shared their second and third experiences of sending their child there. David announced to the group, and to Matthew, "I will never come back here again." And there was never the need to again.

Matthew was given the opportunity to work in a fine restaurant through a contact of close friend, Babs Pruden. There he was coached and encouraged by the chefs and then went on to Johnson Wales Culinary Institute where he completed the Bachelor's degree in restaurant management. His beginning as a chef at The Inn at Turkey Hill in Bloomsburg set him up for 17 years of wonderful experiences in food preparation and repeated four-star ratings.

It was there he interviewed, hired, and married Jenny, his pastry chef. After the birth of daughter Madelyn in 2010, and after Jenny being a third runner-up on the TV show Hell's Kitchen, and after the Inn receiving highest ratings by Open Table, Matthew and Jenny moved to Gilbert, AZ.

Immediate job applications and immediate hiring resulted in Matthew working at the Honor Health Hospital in Scottsdale Arizona. He is the manager of the private catering for the hospital. Jenny quickly moved to a starter job at Kneaders restaurant in their pastry division. And soon after she made contact with and was hired by the Pastry Chef at the Fairmont Princess Hotel

Life in Arizona started with their move to Gilbert to live with me. Madelyn at four was ready for pre-school, and their two dogs, Diego and Daisy, were welcomed by David's and my Zaydie. The Revak family was now expanding in Arizona with the family of three siblings Matthew, Heather and Shally all living here.

Matthew today with Jenny and Madelyn

Chapter 10a
Practice in Bloomsburg

DAVID …

In the middle of my Internship as we were considering settling in York to begin General Practice, I received a call from a pathology resident. He worked with me at Memorial Hospital. He asked if we'd be interested in setting up a practice in Bloomsburg, about 100 miles north of York. The town had recently lost four doctors, and was eager to fill the gap for General Practice. My friend introduced us to Dr Ritmiller, an OB/GYN, and a powerful guy who could get things done. He invited us to visit Bloomsburg, where he wined and dined us, introduced us to everyone in town, and showed us a house and a urology office we could rent to start our practice. The bank agreed to give us whatever we needed to buy a house.

It seemed like a perfect opportunity, and we couldn't find anything wrong with the deal, so we accepted, and made the move to Bloomsburg. Our first home was located outside of town, and we enjoyed furnishing it with our restored auction finds.

We set up our first office in an old mansion downtown, which we rented for $150 a month. The urologists needed it

Mondays until 5:00 p.m. and Thursdays until noon, so we used it the remaining time, often well into the night. We furnished the office with used equipment from a variety of sources; mostly from the deceased doctors.

A Dr. Glukoff had recently died and the Catholic church had all his furniture and equipment. He had been a big guy and a heavy smoker. He would even smoke while seeing his patients. Back in the early seventies, smoking didn't have quite the stigma it does now, and the dangers were just becoming known. Even during hospital staff meetings, everyone would have their cigarette or cigar, and the room would be full of smoke.

The Catholic church called and asked if I needed any office equipment, so I went and took a look. There were examining tables, lights, several pieces of beautiful oak furniture, and many items from the turn of the century. One was an ENT (ear, nose, throat) chair with a swinging glass tray and bowl a patient could spit into. I couldn't use the older stuff in my modern office, but I later put it in the library of an old mansion I bought.

Later, I got a call from the doctor who did the drug and alcohol therapy in town. He said "I think there's a lot of equipment in the basement of one of the clinics I go to."

It had belonged to a Dr. Miller, who had committed suicide. It was good enough for our office, so I took it. We had five or six rooms in our office, and had been needing more furniture and equipment to fill them all.

A year or so later, Dr. Miller's son, who was a dermatologist, called me. He had heard that his father's furniture was stored in the basement of his former office and went to get it. He found out I had bought it, and wondered if he could buy it back. I had him come over and said "Take whatever you want."

I didn't want to charge him for his own father's things, so I just helped him load it up.

When I was growing up in Mt. Carmel, every doctor had a big house with a separate office space. I wanted the same, and could imagine a big mansion with my office in one area and living quarters in another. So when a local surgeon, Dr. Beckley, passed away about a year after we arrived, I was very interested in his place—an all-brick building with living quarters, surgical suites and examining rooms, and a three car garage in the back. It would have been perfect, and I would have loved to buy it. But Blair preferred to keep family life separate from work, and didn't want our office and home to be in the same building. When she went to work and put on her white smock, she was a doctor. But when she was home, she was Mom. So we did not purchase it.

Our practice was building quickly, and we were thinking about branching out. The bank called and asked if we were interested in a building they had in Orangeville, just seven miles away. The town's population was about 900 people, and they had no doctor. We drove over and found a huge building with lots of space, that was perfect for us. We rented part of it to a psychologist, and we had our own lab in another area. From that time on, we usually had two offices, and at one time we had three. In 1973 we built our own office next to the hospital in Bloomsburg, replacing the old house we had been renting.

The lab was a huge convenience for us. We hired a medical technician who worked at each office a couple of days a week. She drew blood from the patients and did the work up in our own lab, and could call us with the results right away. It was twice as fast as getting the work done at the hospital, and cost us half as much.

I loved practicing medicine … loved everything about it. I used to say I wanted to practice into my nineties, although the average doctor retires in his or her fifties.

I thought of the family doctors we'd had when I was growing up; Betsko, Mochinski, Schmegelski and Greco. I remember when Dr. Schmegelski would come to our house to see me when I was ill he would sing out, "Candy, soda, five cents, where's the dipsy doodle kid!"

Dr. Greco had his own lab and lab tech and provided respiratory therapy. At that time, a general practitioner would do everything; deliver babies, perform surgery, set fractures and dislocations, and remove lesions. You knew when you walked into your doctor's office that he was going to help you.

I wanted to be that kind of doctor, and that's what I incorporated into my practice. I knew my patients' names and everything about them. We did it all, including serving as a VD clinic. I delivered over 3500 babies. The total cost when we started practice would be about $150.00 from first visit through delivery. Most everyone paid in cash. Office calls were only five or six dollars, and the patient would leave with the necessary medicine. It wasn't unusual for us to dispense drugs then; but only antibiotics such as Erythromycin, Amoxicillin, and Tetracycline. Prepackaging of prescription pills was just beginning to be developed.

The drug companies would supply us with the drugs, and if we'd buy a certain amount, they'd throw in extra benefits, like a sound system for the office, or some other "luxury" feature.

Our practice grew, we were so busy we recruited Dr. Bill Kuprevich who was from nearby Danville and who became a wonderful partner for us. We practiced together over 30 years and never had a conflict.

After Bill joined us, Blair was nearing thirty and still had that dream of having six children. She became pregnant again. Shally was born in 1973, and we now had three kids under the age of five.

Husband-Wife Doctors Set To Practice Here

A romance that started with a frog's "croak" and culminated in marriage, will shortly blossom into a profesional union in Bloomsburg.

Dr. Revak — both of them — will shortly open offices for medical practice at 326 Market street.

Dr. Blair Revak, an M.D., begins her professional duties here today, joining the medical staff of the Bloomsburg Hospital.

Her husband, Dr. David J. Revak, has five more days to go before he completes his preparation.

How It Started

A native of York, Dr. Blair met her husband-to-be when they were both pre-Med students at Susquehanna University. She recalled that the now "Dr. Dave" h a d n ' t particularly noticed her prior to the day she dropped the frog.

She was studying the effects of a spinal experiment on the frog when it "croaked." She said she became "all excited" and dropped the frog. Until then, he had thought her to be somewhat of a cold scientist. The incident caused him to change his mind and, viola!, romance was born in the laboratory.

Now, five years and two children later, the couple, almost on their anniversary, are ready for practice.

Dr. Blair

"Dr. Blair" is the daughter of Mr. and Mrs. John B. Hoover, of Woodbury, N.J. Her father is a refrigeration engineer in Philadelphia. She is a graduate of Susquehanna, the Women's Medical College of Pennsylvania in 1969 and served as a rotating intern at Germantown Hospital. She was president of her class in medical school for two years.

She will open a practice in general medicine.

Dr. Dave

"Dr. Dave" will practice general medicine and obstetrics. Also an alumnus of Susquehanna, he is a graduate of Philadelphia College of Osteopathic Medicine and is a few short days from completi his internship at York Memori Osteopathic Hospital.

He is the son of Mr. a Mrs. John Revak of 240 Ea Avenue, Mt. Carmel. His fath is a printer for the Shamok News Dispatch.

Still a Shortage

The couple plans to open fices on Market street, abc mid-July. Their arrival here w somewhat alleviate a curre critical shortage of physicia (Continued on Page Nine)

DOCTORS BLAIR AND DAVID REVAK

in the area. The Bloomsburg Hospital and the Columbia County Medical Society both cooperated in enlisting their interest in coming here.

The doctors have secured a residence on Bloomsburg R.D. 3, in the "Wonderview" development. They have two children, a daughter, Heather, two, and a son, Matthew, five months old. Both doctors are members of the Lutheran Church.

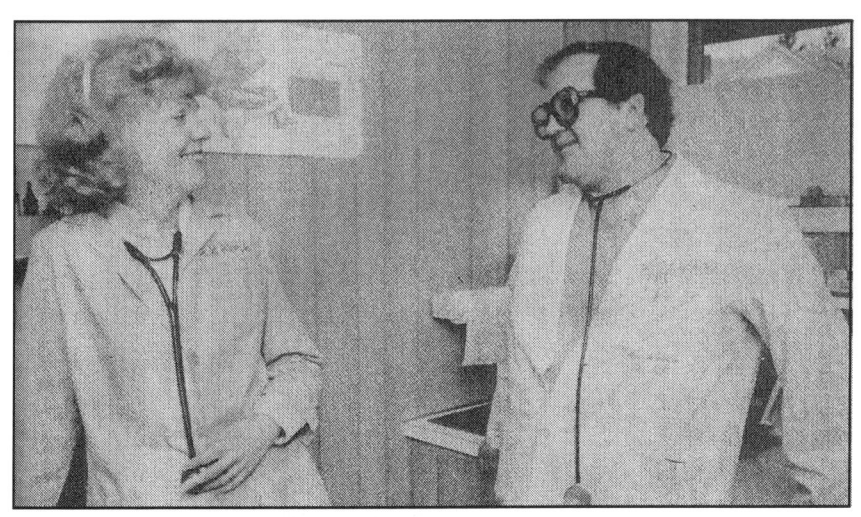

Early days of practice

First house in Bloomsburg
Front (above)   Back (below)

Chapter 10b
Shally

"Do you like my new shoes?"

Blair ...
If you had met David just a bit before this occasional question you may have been somewhat aware of his humor but not prepared for the question he had for you. David's humor left many standing, caught off guard. As I have shared often, it probably was a main reason our marriage survived all those years. A potentially inflammatory situation could be easily softened by a crazy comment from him. And as the recipient of his comments (especially me) broke into laughter, there's no feeling of anger left.

David was clothing conscious, especially as it related to his opportunity to make a statement. He started to wear painters' pants in the '60s, long before they were the fashion, and he took credit for starting that fad.

His mom made me aware of the issues I had before me when we announced our plans to marry. I had known David nearly a year and knew he never wore socks, no matter the dress, he thought socks were too much of a bother. But life took a new look when his conservative, often very silent, mother, Anna, blurted to me in a pre-marital warning, "Well, I hope you can get him to wear underwear."

When he was spending great numbers of hours in the operating room and delivery room, the most convenient shoes became wooden clogs. Clogs were approved for the operating room when he started the habit (never to be followed by anyone, incidentally) and they became his trademark. The knocking of wooden clogs during his early morning rounds to visit patients announced, "Dr. David is here!" as he entered the floor. A woman in labor knew it was okay to push as the wooden click hit the long hallway of the OB department.

Sometimes it was hard to find a new pair, and though we didn't have the internet, we had shoe-knowing people searching the world for a pair of wooden clogs. When David, retired the OB nurses got an old pair of his clogs and had them decorated for his retirement gift.

Among David's ventures into footwear, the 1970s brought the fad of roller skates. David knew patients confined to the hospital for holidays were very sad. To liven the environment, he wore rollerblades to make his rounds and cheered up the crowds even in the Intensive Care Unit.

After returning from the west in 1983, he was a daily wearer of cowboy boots. The collection grew from regular cowhide to iguana and some boots engineered from a boa constrictor snake.

That venture into the fashion industry led to his "do you like my new shoes?" line. He frequently wore elastic waist shorts, and loose fitting jeans even served him well. In a spontaneous step toward his victim he would pull his waistband forward inviting a look, and inquire "do you like my new shoes?" And as the person facing him started to respond with a tilt of the head they would catch themselves, quickly jumping backward and responding with a spontaneous laugh.

"How did I get caught in that trick?" was often their unspoken reaction. I must say that there were many times in our lives that a spontaneous question, completely out of context and completely unrelated, created for us a similar thought-diverting laugh.

Shally would be considered the "fashion-knowing" member of the family. Why that came to her is not to my clear understanding, but her dad certainly gave it permission to stand out. She, like her dad, never worried over the choice of being different. In fourth grade she requested an afro hair permanent and proudly wore it. It adorned her head when the local press came to her school and photographed her seated beside Eric Wise for a press release about a school project. Little did we know then that the two of them would begin dating at age 17 and continue to a marriage that now exceeds 18 years.

I think Shally was about 15 when she gave Joe, the wildest hairstylist in town, free reign, and sported her own Mohawk. Another time a shaved checkerboard decorated both sides of her head. To this day new hairstyles speak Shally's separate voice.

I was so afraid I'd be too old to bear a child when at the age of 30 I announced to David, "we must have this second pregnancy soon."

At that time in the medical community, a first pregnancy at 35 was considered an elderly primagravida and clearly, I was now approaching that elderly age. So pregnancy it was.

Heather had been delivered under the gun of multiple drugs and a spinal anesthesia. I was ready for the natural movement. David ruptured my membranes at home and then had to have dinner and rest even as my contractions immediately became active. Finally, we ventured to the hospital. I was feeling rejected when he had a private patient also in labor and followed both of us into the delivery rooms. He did deliver Shally with Dr. Corson, the head of the Department of Obstetrics, in the Bloomsburg Hospital. Clark made the courtesy attendance to my delivery, at my request, should there be a problem. Dr. Corson always signed out to David when out of town. He trusted David to a great degree, even asking him to be the delivering doctor for his own first grandchild.

A very calm baby, Shally nursed for three months before I returned to work. Elsie had been a patient of mine. She was near retirement when I asked her to help with the three kids for a committed three months. She was easily available, as she told me she did not have enough paid in to Social Security to collect retirement, so I offered to hire her for that three months so she could contribute to her retirement fund and collect.

She and husband Dan stayed on as part of our extended family for seven years. Dan died of a heart attack at our house and Elsie could not return without him in her life. Though all three kids were in school, I still looked to find someone to help with caring for the kids, and managing our schedule of night call, deliveries, meetings and meals.

When Shally was an infant I requested full Medical Staff privileges at the hospital and was denied by the staff, as I could not attend the 7 a.m. meetings, having three children under five years. My, how life changed, when 16 years later a new male member of the staff announced he could not attend those same meetings, as he had to take his kids to the school bus. I was Chief of Staff and with a spontaneous reflex, responded, "get a life, this is part of the duty". The meeting times were adjusted to accommodate his schedule. This was 1991 not 1973!

Shally was the baby of the family. She has always been the peacemaker and family "solver" when there was conflict. She, like Heather, was interested in sports and was an excelling student. When Celestia and Charles joined us, Shally became the intermediary in kid issues. And I soon learned the expanded mechanisms of larger families. You/Mom can't do it all when the family population exceeds three children, a caregiver told me. Shally now had two sisters to play games and help her with assignments, clothes and bedtime conversations.

High school basketball, track, soccer and tennis occupied much of Shally's non-school time. David loved to share the story of Shally's tennis escapade with a young woman who was number 1 in the district, and for whom Shally was a nemesis as she challenged her position. David attended many matches, as he was in the treatment of his Hodgkin's Disease when Shally was in high school, and he had more free time.

During a challenging match, the other girl called the ball out on several occasions that clearly were inside the line. Shally stopped the game and walked to the net, calling her competitor to her for conversation. Sitting nearby, David heard his daughter say, "You don't have to cheat, you are better than me, be honest." The girl dropped her head, walked to her baseline and stayed honest after that.

Eric and Shally began dating in 11th grade. Eric is six months younger than Shally. Recently they shared the story of when he got his permit and his dad took him to learn to drive. His dad said, "Boy, you really did well for your first time changing gears."

No, he told me, he didn't tell his dad the real reason he could change gears so well. Shally had taught Eric to drive on her car months before. She said she was just passing it on as Heather had taught her to drive when she was still only 14.

Shally's soccer career was with the high school and a select team. Travels to Denmark to play in a tournament gave her a visit to the original Legoland. She was recruited by colleges for soccer and chose Elizabethtown to play soccer, though there was no scholarship money with that. She transferred back home and attended Bloomsburg University. Heavy class schedules kept her from playing soccer beyond her first year there.

I, as a mother, have many good soccer memories, as I coached her team when she was 11 years old as a last minute request from the AYSO director, who said they desperately needed a coach for the team. These kids had played soccer more than four years. I had never played and had some quick learning to do to even know what an on-sides play was and to know how to identify it. As it turned out, we defeated a team at the end of the season which was destined—according to their coach—to be undefeated. We heard championship trophies had already been purchased. And we, my team, beat them. I had a lot of coaching advice from my players all season. Running off the field, Kevin would say, "Coach, do this" or "Coach, put him there." And we had a lot of celebration to share.

Basketball made a guard out of Shally. She was shorter than her basketball sister, Heather, by four inches. She held the record for percentage of successful foul shots at Central High School until 2008 that we know of.

Track included the sprint runs, and a rare long distance run. Such preparation was valuable, as she is now, as an adult mother, competing in many varieties of runs including a recent mini-triathalon. She conditions by swimming with me at the clubhouse while I am in water aerobics with friends. She also runs and bikes with many of her friends. She and Eric are strongly tied to physical conditioning and enjoyment of those conditioning sports. Skiing and hiking are favorite family sports. Jesse makes it clear to me, though, that he is a snowboarder, not a skier.

Shally and Eric married in 1997. She chose the wedding over the house down payment (each child had that as a choice) and had a wonderful celebration. And it was at the toast to the wedding couple that David proudly announced how she was conceived under the Christmas tree as part of my plan to be pregnant before I was 31. Any of our kids can speak to that quote about Dad: "You don't have to be worried about embarrassing yourself when you are with Dad, he does it for himself."

With the marriage, Shally and Eric decided to join Heather and Adam in Arizona. Eric did recreational therapy with disabled folks, having graduated from Penn State with that degree. He did river rafting and movies among many wonderful giving occasions. Shally began work with a Payless store as a manager. After only one year in Arizona they decided to return to the roots of their love in Pennsylvania. Three years later they chose to return to Arizona.

Now their lives had grown. Shally was working as a financial aid trainer for University of Phoenix in Philadelphia, and transferred to that role in Phoenix. Eric went on to enrich his career with some type of computer certification and moved to work with the University of Phoenix online software staff.

On their return to Arizona they lived in our Gilbert house while we lived and worked in Peach Springs on the Hualapai Reservation. We had retired from our practice and were planning to extend our work experience on various reservations, starting in South Dakota. Our Health insurance availability had expired and we needed coverage.

After two years being locum tenens with the Hualapai at Peach Springs, we obtained work when they opened the new Peach Springs Clinic. We decided to stay in the RV 30 miles from Peach Springs. After two years of RV living and weekend visits to the Valley, we bought a house. Our permanence in Peach Springs and the Kingman area lasted another three years.

Then David had more trouble with his lungs, including several episodes of coughing blood. I wanted us to be nearer more advanced health care, and we had truly exhausted the experience there. We now had Medicare, so we retired to the valley.

Shally delivered baby boy Jesse in 2004. She had called to tell me she was bitten by a bug and I was already medically diagnosing an anxious body reaction when she said, "I changed my mind about kids, I want to have a baby." In no time, Jesse was coming into the world. It was another surprise to all of us when Amaya came on the scene 13 months later. Now at 9 and 11, they are special kids who live near me.

Shally & Eric
June 21, 1997

*The Wise Family:
Jesse, Amaya, Eric, Shally*

Chapter 10c
More about Practice in Bloomsburg

DAVID ...

Blair saw patients and handled the business side of the practice. We worked together and made rounds together for four years, except when she was having kids. We were always busy. My typical workday was from 7:00 a.m. to 8:00 p.m., but it wouldn't be unusual for me to go in at 5:00 a.m. and stay until the following 2:00 a.m. I'd sometimes work alone, and my mind was always looking at how to do things better. Most doctors were still using three-by-five cards to keep their patient information. I wanted something more efficient, so we designed our own charts, similar to what is being used today.

While working our busy practice, we were both also on staff at the Bloomsburg Hospital, and I served as the physician for some of the high school and college teams. Blair was involved in the local family planning clinic, the women's trauma center, and served on the school board for a while. Neither of us had much spare time.

Spending so much time together could have become a problem, but somehow we made it work. We respected one another and allowed the other to grow. It also helped that we both had our own outside interests. Even though our personalities were very different, we complemented each other and worked well together.

The long hours, no time off, and my periods of working alone began taking their toll. After Dr. Bill Kuprevich joined our practice, I was able to take every other weekend off, unless I was called to deliver a baby.

As in any medical practice, lawsuits were always a problem. My partner, Bill, was sued four times. In one instance, he had a patient who smoked, ate too much and was a heavy drinker. The patient didn't have much money, and for years Bill had been treating him and giving him his medicines for free. Bill had him on a treadmill to monitor his heart, and didn't like what he saw. Since the guy didn't have money, Bill referred him to an internist who wouldn't charge him much. Later, the guy had a heart attack, became debilitated, and sued Bill for not referring him to a specialist for bypass surgery. The guy had no money, not a pot to piss in, and Bill had taken care of him for years for nothing, but he sued and came out with a big settlement.

In another case, Bill and I were both sued. A girl in premature labor came in and delivered right away. I caught the baby and handed it to Bill. It was so tiny, weighing barely over a pound. We sent it to the medical center, where they found it was handicapped, blind, and plagued with other problems—one that required surgery. We occasionally saw the mother and baby in our office over the next few years, and during one of their visits, Blairanne noticed that the woman was badly battered, which may have been the cause of the early delivery. Five or six years after the child's birth, the medical board was doing an investigation into a doctor at the medical center. Lawyers came into our office, and went through every case he'd ever had a problem with. They found that he had operated on that baby, though at that time he did not yet have a license to practice in Pennsylvania. That was enough for a lawsuit. Bill and I were each sued for a million dollars, and the medical center for about five million. And all I had done was catch the baby.

The medical center was also involved in a case where I was sued and I wasn't even around! I was out of town, and had another doctor covering me. He saw a baby that I had previously delivered, and referred the case to the medical center. The baby ended up with brain damage and the medical center was sued, along with the doctor who referred the baby. I was included because I had a doctor cover me who had no insurance. I had to kick in $100,000 and I wasn't even there. I was just thankful I had insurance that covered the lawsuits.

One of my patients was Adam Guzinski, a very angry man who'd had a hard life. He'd had to go underground in Poland to survive the war before immigrating to the U.S., where he settled in Pennsylvania. He bought a farm, but drove to Bethlehem Steel every day to work, then returned home at night and worked the farm. He and his Russian wife fought constantly, and he was a very unhappy man.

I happened to be with him when he had a heart attack. I worked on him for about an hour, and was able to resuscitate him. He remained unconscious until a couple of weeks later, when he woke up and asked, "Why did you bring me back? When I died, I left my body and was going toward a blue light. I saw friends who died during war and saw some of my family, and they were all glad to see me. Then I stopped and turned around. I was on top of the TV, and I saw you pounding on my chest. I said, 'Leave me alone, let me go.' I didn't like the way I was living, I wanted to go."

He was even angry that I had saved his life!

But a couple of weeks later I saw his wife, who said he was a different person. He was nicer, he smiled more, had started going to church, and was making amends with people he'd hurt. He gave up his stressful job and got on disability. I'd see him now and then, and he really was like a different person. He talked to me several times about dying and coming back, and what he'd seen during his "death."

Sadly, a couple of years later, his wife found him dead under their car where he'd been doing repairs.

In 1976 we moved to 101 N. Market Street. Our "new" home was a wonderful old 5,000 square-foot mansion, built in 1805. It had a huge living room, a den, two kitchens, five bedrooms, a back stairway, and a cupola on the roof. Arches were scattered throughout, which we used for storage. I would later remodel a child's room that was next to the master bedroom, turning it into a closet and dressing room for Blair. The house also had a basement, though it was unusable. A stream ran through the property, and seasonal rains regularly sent water flowing into the cellar, turning its dirt floor into a muddy bog.

Still, it was a very unique house, and we paid only $52,000 for it and all its contents.

I loved our new home, but it took us through a lot of highs and lows during the years we owned it. The owner, a gay man whose last name was "Reber," had an "R" engraved or monogrammed on many items, and so we felt fortunate that our name was "Revak" and could put the things to good use. However, before we could take possession, the man's former partner went in and stole much of the contents we had paid for. We eventually retrieved some of the items, but not all.

I still liked going to auctions, and spent many Saturday mornings at sales all over Pennsylvania. I

101 N. Market Street
Above, Circa 1928
Right, 1976

bought furniture, washstands, crocks, jugs, and antiques of any kind. I picked up a lot of medical instruments, and old leather-bound medical books from the mid-1800s. At the end of the auction, anything left over went into the "nickel" pile, and I'd buy all of those too. I bought so much stuff that the auctioneers thought I was a dealer.

Our old house had a beautiful library, which I turned into my own antique medical equipment museum. It included an examining table, an old chair, and a display cabinet with antique medical implements. Some of the items I had purchased from the deceased doctors ended up here, along with many of my auction finds.

When the library's old tin roof began leaking, I went into the attic to seal the holes with tar. While up there, I stumbled across some old boxes filled with even more treasures. I discovered medical books from the 1850s and '60s, a civil war kit, and a document signed by Abraham Lincoln, which I still have today.

I learned a lot about antiques, and through researching the various kinds of wood furniture, I got to know the Amish. Soon, I was delivering some of their babies. Word got out, and before long, all the Amish were coming to me.

We loved the house, enjoyed entertaining, and had lots of parties while we lived there. In 1981, our lives took a different direction, and so we left our charming home, but only temporarily ... or so we thought.

Chapter 11
Crownpoint

DAVID ...

Our practice was doing well, and we loved our old home, but we were both ready for something new and different. Blair had always wanted to work on an Indian reservation, and the more she brought it up over the years, the more interested I became. Initially, we talked about doing two-week stints, covering for other doctors on vacation. But I thought, if we were going to learn anything about the Indian culture, it would take more than two weeks. So in the fall of 1980, we applied for full-time positions with the Indian Health Services.

The following April we attended a conference of the American Medical Students Association in Bismarck, North Dakota. It was an opportunity for us to find out more about the program, and it was also a screening process to determine if we would be a good fit. The interviews were held at Ft. Abraham Lincoln, the post Custer left when he headed off to Little Big Horn, never to return. The day we were there, the wind was blowing at 70 miles an hour; so hard we could barely walk upright, and it was so cold that we considered never returning!

But the prospect of serving on a reservation for a couple of years still appealed to us, and at least it wouldn't be near Bismarck. We learned that there were ten healthcare centers, built and run by the government, scattered throughout Navajo land. Each one served people within a 150+ mile radius, and operated in cooperation with the Indian Health Services. Though the IHS was at first leery about taking us, wondering why we would give up a good practice to work on a reservation, once they got to know us, we were hired. I had to join the Army as non-uniform military, and was given the rank of Major, while Blair became part of the civil service.

Soon after being accepted, we spent a weekend flying to four different sites in Arizona and New Mexico, to determine where we wanted to practice. A couple of places were extremely remote, and we didn't want to be that far away from everything. As it was, the site we chose—Crown point, New Mexico—was still 90 miles from a grocery store. But it was on the reservation, providing more day-to-day contact with the Indian people, which was in tune with our goals. The hospital at Crownpoint was a 35-bed facility that served 16,000 people.

We returned to Bloomsburg and made preparations to report on July 1, 1981. The practice would continue on, in the hands of our partner, Dr. Bill Kuprevich and other associates..

We wanted to keep our home and possibly return to it in two years, so we decided to rent it during our absence. We packed up all the antiques, books, tools and other valuables into old trunks, and stashed it all in a room in the attic, adding a padlock to the door.

Our kids were now 12, 10 and 7, and not too sure about this new move. When we promised new adventures and painted an exciting picture of the west, complete with Indians and horses and a family dog, they began to perk up.

We had barely arrived at our new home, when we realized we had a lot of adjusting to do. The environment, the people and even our schedule were all foreign to us. The Navajo reservation was 60 miles north of Gallup, in an area known as Crownpoint, New Mexico. The landscape was unlike anything we had known, and took some getting used to. Instead of green rolling hills, and meandering rivers, we were faced with stark, dry desert. Trees were replaced with cactus and scrub brush that tried to pass for something more.

We also had to adjust to the Navajo people, who didn't trust whites. They seldom had much to say even in the best of circumstances ... and we didn't see them during the best. It wasn't long before I was asking myself, "What's the grandson of Russian and Slovakian immigrants doing living with Indians in the middle of the desert?"

The Indians also needed to adapt to us, though they usually chose not to. Some previous doctors had gained a bad reputation, and we were all judged by them. Many were fresh out of medical school and had to pay back their tuition by serving on a reservation. They were young and inexperienced, and worse, would try to impose their own values on the Native Americans, considering them stupid and backward. It was a shame they couldn't see the harm they were doing.

As a result, the Indians didn't trust us, remaining suspicious of the white man's ways, and preferring to consult with their own medicine men, seeing us only as a last resort.

The Indians believe that illness is the result of being out of tune with nature and the universe, and that the medicine men could put them back in balance. I treated one heart patient who had run out of his medication and was filling with fluid; but he was covered with ashes, herbs and flowers from a traditional healing ceremony.

We learned that there is a hierarchy of medicine men: star gazers, hand tremblers, crystal gazers and herbalists. The hand tremblers didn't touch their patients, they just chanted over them. The herbalists were the very lowest form, and we were considered herbalists, because we gave out pills. Interestingly, the medicine men were usually wise, and understood their limits. If they knew they couldn't help someone with herbs and communal sings, they referred them to us.

Their healers had a strange looking suction cup that they'd put on the patient's abdomen, leaving a big bruise. When we saw that bruise on a patient, we knew they had seen the medicine man before coming to us. One woman told us her gall bladder had been removed by the medicine man—non surgically. When we did the gall bladder study afterward, there was nothing there.

The medicine men were allowed to come in to the clinic, but they wouldn't talk to us. They spoke only to the patients, and only in Navajo. When we were there in the early 1980s, Navajo was still the most spoken language on the isolated reservations, and we had interpreters translate for those coming to the clinic. Now, very few of the younger people speak Navajo, and English has taken over, although there is a push to preserve the native language ... at least within the tribe.

Our working environment and schedule required another adjustment. Before we left Bloomsburg, we had been working 80 hours a week, which had begun to seem normal. We arrived at the reservation and learned that our hours with the Indian Health Services would be considerably less. The days were short, and we rarely worked nights or weekends. We saw patients from 8:00 to 11:15 a.m., and then again 1 to 4:30pm. We could only work when the clinic was open, and IHS determined when the clinic would be open.

Superstitions, as they were labeled by the white man, or traditional culture to the Navajo were standard protocols on the reservation. We learned and participated in those we were able to. If we shaved any body parts—to give an IV, for example—or even shaved a baby's head, we had to give the hair to family. They believed that spells could be put on the shaven hair, and if anyone else gained possession, it could be used in bad way.

Another cultural standard revolved around the medicine bag—similar to a lucky charm in our society. One of the nurses on the reservation needed to have her gall bladder removed, so Blair sent her to hospital for surgery. As she was going into surgery, she developed significant arrhythmia, and the surgery was cancelled. After she had been home a couple of days, she came to our house to talk to Blair. She said, "I want to tell you why I didn't get the surgery. When we go into any stressful situation, we have to have our medicine bag with us. They wouldn't let me take it into the operating room. As soon as they took it away from me, I started to feel my heart fluttering, and they stopped my surgery."

Blair talked to her for quite a while, trying to convince her to go back, but she refused. Then Blair suggested, "How about if we work out a way for you to take it in with you?"

The nurse was adamant that she would not go back, and she didn't. Thankfully, she ended up doing okay without the surgery.

Our patients often came from 70 or 80 miles away. Most disease and injuries were related to the land in some way: broken bones from falls, back pains from sheep shearing, or hepatitis from poor sanitary conditions. Many of the diseases were infectious, and so could be cured, unlike the heart disease and cancer we saw so much of in Bloomsburg.

Because of the distance most of our patients traveled, we found we often had time to care successfully for them if they made it to the clinic. We'd say, "If the patient can make it to us, we can save their life."

We did just about everything medical that could be done, and treated some cases that we hadn't had to deal with in Bloomsburg. FOBPU was one of those. Our first night on duty, Blair saw a kid who came in covered with bumps, scrapes, cuts and bruises. At the time, she'd never seen injuries quite like his before, but we soon learned that they were very common on the reservation, and were caused when the victim "Fell Off Back of Pick Up," abbreviated on the charts as FOBPU. Another of the kids in that accident was flown to Albuquerque Medical Center with a bleed inside his head and was returned to us for continuing care after they put monitors in his head.

Life on the reservation provided more than the usual number of alcohol-related accidents and trauma. One of the worst we handled was a truck rollover with five kids in the back. Two were killed outright when the truck rolled over them. Another one, a heavy kid, was still alive and brought in to the clinic. When we began removing his coat so that we could start an IV, all his intestines spilled out onto the table. The truck had rolled over him too, bursting his insides.

A drunk Indian is a dangerous Indian—to himself just as often as to others. One guy with a death wish poured gasoline on himself and lit a match. He was burned everywhere except his feet—saved by his cowboy boots—and his butt crack. We learned that he had shot himself in the head three years earlier and survived, but he seemed to be intent on suicide. All we could do was send him to the burn center. He survived again, but his hands had burned off, and he couldn't see or talk. He did eventually die a year or so later.

That brings to mind the alcohol issue that was often the case in emergencies. One night years later, when we were working in the canyon caring for the Havasupai tribe, a very drunk Havasupai Indian was brought in with about 23 stab wounds, inflicted by his black girlfriend. He was so covered with blood that I couldn't see where the wounds were, so I stripped him down and pushed him in the clinic's shower. He sat there butt-ass naked while I stripped myself down to shorts and sneakers. I used the shower hose to try and rinse off all the blood from the wounds in his belly, his genitals, his neck and head. I washed his long hair, which reached halfway down his back and was matted with blood. I was getting soaking wet during this process, and the cop who brought the guy in stood there watching and laughing at me.

I said, "Well, it's the only way I can see where all these wounds are; he's covered with blood, mud and dirt."

I finally got his hair clean and tied it up, then got him out and had him lay on an examining table. He was drunk and naked, and I was soaking wet in my underwear and sneakers. The cop said, "I'm going to the office for a minute."

I said, "No problem, he's sleeping. I'm gonna sew up some of these wounds."

I felt his stomach, trying to determine if it had been punctured. It was hard to tell, because there was a huge layer of fat over his belly. If any of the wounds had reached into his abdomen, they would have caused internal bleeding. Evidently, the girlfriend used a short-bladed knife, and my friend seemed to be doing okay. I took his blood pressure and checked his vitals. It looked like the only thing that saved him was the fact that he was quite fat, and the knife wounds never reached his vital organs.

By now it was two o'clock in the morning, and I decided to at least get my pants on. I went into the other room and had just gotten one leg in my pants, when the Indian went flying out the door ... butt-ass naked.

I dropped my pants on the floor and took off after him. There we were; a naked Indian running through the village, and me—a respected doctor—chasing after him in my scivvies. It was a good thing he was drunk and stumbling, because I was getting short of breath. I could just imagine people hearing the commotion, looking out their windows, and thinking, "What the hell is going on! There's Dr. Revak in his underwear chasing a butt-ass naked Indian through the village!"

I finally caught up and grabbed him by the hair, yelling, "What's the matter with you!"

About this time the cop rode up on an ATV and said, "Get him the hell on here."

I shoved him on the back of the ATV and we all went back to the clinic, where I finished tending his wounds. Since most weren't deep, I covered them with antiseptic, applied steri-strips, bandaged him up, and gave him some antibiotics. By this time it was almost 5:00 a.m. and I was exhausted. A helicopter usually came in around 7:00 or 8:00 in the morning, and I was going to make sure my patient was on it.

The cop got on the chopper with him, and they took off for the Flagstaff hospital. About noon, the cop called and said, "I got news for you, I took him into the ER, went for coffee, and when I went back he was gone."

About four days later, our guy was found drunk in downtown Flagstaff and taken to jail. Five months afterward, he walked into our clinic. He'd lost about sixty pounds while in jail, and I didn't recognize him right away.

I did a quick check of his vitals, and found that his diabetes was under control and his blood pressure was normal. We often joked that jail was the best thing for the Indians. They'd eat healthier, lose weight, and keep their blood pressure reigned in. It was the best treatment for the diabetes that was so prevalent among the Indians.

Not having learned his lesson, he went back to his girlfriend. She stabbed him again, and they both ended up back in jail.

Whether alcohol induced, or just general craziness, many of the local residents would occasionally go nuts. We had only been there a couple of months when Blair called me at the hospital and said, "You'd better get over here, 'cause this guy's running around the neighborhood with an axe and acting crazy." It was the man who lived right behind us, and he was going after dogs and cats, and even threatening people with his axe.

Snake and insect bites were common, and could often be dangerous. One poor guy was bitten on the testicles by a brown recluse spider while sitting in the outhouse. He survived, but couldn't walk well and twitched a lot afterward.

One of the saddest cases was the call to help a four-year-old child who had been trapped in an abandoned refrigerator. But the call came too late ... the child had died.

Although either of us could take care of just about anything that came along, Blair was the obstetrics and mental health specialist, while my focus was as the TB, VD and infectious disease specialist. We delivered a lot of the babies, including the New Year's babies for 1982 and '83.

I took care of normal deliveries, but those women requiring C-sections were sent the 60 miles to Gallup. There was one patient who wouldn't deliver, and I knew she needed a C-section. We put her in an ambulance and I went along to monitor her blood pressure and vitals. The ambulance hit a huge bump, we both flew into the air, and I came back down on top of her. Fortunately, my fall didn't make things any worse for her.

Another woman had been in labor for ten to twelve hours, and the baby just wouldn't come down. Again, we planned to send her to Gallup for a C-section, but her family insisted on having a Medicine Man come in. When he arrived I was sent outside the room, where I stood peeking around the door frame, watching the proceedings. My first observation was that while I was in sterile scrubs and booties, he was in there wearing muddy boots with cow shit on them.

He began chanting and holding his hands over the woman's belly, then gave her something to sip on while he chanted. I had no idea what she was sipping, but ten or twenty minutes later, she began panting, and the baby just shot out. It could've been a coincidence, or there might have been something to the chanting and the magic potion in the cup. You never know.

Our kids were also having to make adjustments to this new life in the desert. They had left their friends behind, and now were on an Indian reservation where—not only did they not know anyone—but for the first time in their lives, they were the minority! They were picked on by the Indian kids, and had a tough time feeling comfortable in school. I told Heather to choose the biggest of the kids picking on her and beat her up.

We lived in a house trailer next to the clinic, in a compound with other Anglos; mostly teachers, clinic employees and hospital workers. There were a few other non-Navajo children around, but very few. One of those was Adam, the son of a nurse at the clinic. Several years later, Adam would become Heather's husband.

The reservation offered very little in the way of entertainment, especially for the kids. There was little TV and not much in the way of radio reception. There were no movie theaters, skating rinks, or even school sports; opportunities we had taken for granted at home.

Since there wasn't much for kids to do on the reservation, we bought a couple of cheap horses for them. I had met a cowboy from Colorado, who quickly became a life-long buddy, and he helped the kids develop their riding skills.

We rented a pasture away from the housing area, and kept the horses there when we weren't riding. We had to keep the fences repaired and make sure the animals had hay and grain. After a while, we added a third horse. I'd drive to the pasture and ride one horse back to the house, leading the other two for the kids to ride. They loved owning and riding horses in the "wild west." When the mares had foals, we gave them away in exchange for grain and hay.

One of the Indians had a wild Palomino and said, "If you can catch it, I'll sell it to you for $100." My buddy, Bill, caught him for me and we kept him in our small back yard. Bill assured us he'd be riding it in a week, and he was true to his word. Now we had four horses, and bought a four-horse stock trailer. But the Palomino, though beautiful, was nasty and not good around the kids. He had kicked both Heather and me, so we decided to get rid of him, and traded him for three saddles and $50.00 cash.

Besides the horses, we looked for other ways to entertain ourselves. We cooked and baked and spent a lot of time together as a family, often playing Parcheesi and Monopoly. I put in a horseshoe pit, and everybody would come to our place to pitch horseshoes and drink beer. It was supposed to be dry on the reservation, but we always managed to have beer.

We were on call every fourth weekend, but on most of our free weekends, we would take off somewhere, often camping in national parks. We were always surprised at how little-used the park campgrounds were. At home we had to have reservations to make sure we got a spot; out here, there were no crowds. When we weren't camping, we spent our off weekends shopping in Albuquerque, or exploring as far as Phoenix. We realized life on the reservation was hard on the kids, and did whatever we could to keep them happy and entertained.

Matthew and Adam became friends. Just within the last couple of years, Adam has told stories of things he and Matthew did back then … things we didn't know about at the time. They went out at night with BB guns, shooting out all the lights, and would sometimes lay in ambush for Indian kids, and shoot BBs at them.

Both Matthew and Heather fell behind in school. In hindsight, we wish we had home-schooled them. Shally had no problem because she was only in first grade. Her biggest problem was that the other kids ignored her on the playground. She and a black kid were the only non-Navajo in her class. The teacher was amazed at how well-adjusted Shally was, despite the fact that she was in the minority. But her personality is that of an outgoing, social, peacemaker. She just makes things work; and so she did well academically, and eventually acquired several good Navajo friends.

We expected to find discrimination against whites on the Navajo reservation, but were surprised to learn how far their prejudice went. The Navajo call themselves "Dine" meaning "the only people." They believe that no one of any other ethnic group matters: not whites, blacks, or even other Indians.

The administrative assistant for the clinic was an Arapahoe-Cheyenne Indian. Most people—Navajo and whites alike—didn't like him. He was mean, a manipulator, and was diddling the help. He seemed to have a particular axe to grind with us. We thought the reason was that Blair was seeing his wife in the clinic on a regular basis. He didn't like the fact that Blair was involved in his life and knew so much about what went on in his home. So I think he tried to make our lives miserable.

We had our horses out in the canyon, and I'd bring them to the house and saddle them so the kids could ride. We couldn't leave anything out at the corral, so I would take the saddles off at home and lock them in our garage. He decided that we shouldn't be allowed to bring the horses to our house, and took his complaint to the housing committee. They voted against him, but he decided to enforce "his" rules anyway.

He started coming over and hassling the kids, who were all under age 13. A typical bully. I saw him giving them a hard time one day and went to his house, about a block away. I said, "What's the matter with you? What are you trying to prove? I have a garden, and if the horses poop, I put it in my garden. We ride them and take them back to the corral. What is the problem?"

"You just can't do it," he said.

I said, "And you just can't hassle my kids. You got a problem, you hassle me."

He said, "What are you going to do about it?"

"Keep it up, and you'll be the first Indian to be scalped in the last 100 years," I told him.

He said, "You think you're big enough?"

That's when I went after him. He jumped the fence, ran into his house and called the cops.

Blair got called out of clinic and was told, "The police are at your house to arrest your husband."

It wasn't quite that dire. Two Navajo policemen—I knew both—showed up on our doorstep and asked, "What happened? Did you threaten him?"

I wasn't going lie to them, so I said, "No I didn't threaten him, I *promised* him that if he ever hassled my kids again, he would be the first Indian in a hundred years to be scalped."

The cops didn't like him any more than we did, and one said to me, "Make sure you kill him first."

He lost that battle, but he found a way to get back at us. Part of his job responsibility was approving all the financial vouchers, and it wasn't long before we stopped getting our travel vouchers and educational reimbursements, which hurt us financially.

I'd had enough, and said to Blair, "I'm leaving!"

She reminded me that we couldn't leave, because we had a two-year commitment. All of this was causing a lot of stress in our marriage, so I volunteered to go to South Dakota for a month and let things cool down.

In February, I went to South Dakota and served as their Clinical Director. I actually had a good time there, and got to know some interesting people. The ophthalmologist was a burned out druggie from Haight-Ashbury, but a good surgeon; the anesthesiologist was from Ecuador, by way of Philadelphia; and the surgeon was just out of rehab for alcoholism. They were all really nice guys, and the four of us ran that clinic for a month.

We were in a place where most Indian Health workers did not want to go. The Sioux Indians are tougher than nails, and we were handling stabbings, shootings, automobile accidents ... it was trauma up the gazoo! In one accident, a woman went all the way through her windshield. The surgeon operated on her and was able to get her fixed up. It was an interesting month in that regard, but when there weren't traumas, it could be boring.

I was alone, missing Blair, and it was 20 below zero ... too cold to get out and do anything—even if there had been anything to do. So I kept myself busy getting the clinic cleaned up and put in order. I got all the charts up to date and made sure the pharmacy was squared away. When the month was over, I received a commendation for getting the clinic back in shape.

I went back to Crownpoint, and realized that nothing had changed there. I often became frustrated with the bureaucracy of the Indian Health Services, and the silly rules of the Army. Plans and projects were researched, discussed, and voted on, but nothing ever came of them. The meetings seemed to be a waste of time, and I began to ignore them, which got me in hot water with my superior officers. My attitude was, "Why should I attend a meeting to vote on something that's not going to happen?" The Army didn't quite see it my way, but nothing came of it.

Our house in Bloomsburg had been rented out, but months had gone by with no rent money coming in. We took action to evict the tenants, and shortly afterward, got word that the house had burned down. All we could think about were the antiques we had left behind in the locked store room.

Blair asked her father to go look at the house—especially where the store room had been—looking for remnants of anything that might have escaped the fire. He found nothing—not even the charred ruins of the iron and metal pieces that should have been there. We concluded the renters had stolen everything and then burned the house to hide the theft.

Fortunately, we had insured everything, and eventually received a check for $109,000. We arranged to have what was left of the house boarded up, not knowing if we would try to rebuild. When a realtor called and made an offer, we decided to sell. The realtor remodeled it and sold it to a dentist who used it for an office and apartments. It was a benefit as it was considered in the historic district.

We warned the new owners not to do anything to the basement because of the flooding that came with the rains. The contractor ignored the warnings, and cemented the floor during the remodel. When the first big rain hit, the water had nowhere to go, and the basement was flooded. They had to use a jackhammer on it, and put in sump pumps.

Blair ...
We had traveled to Durango for a ski trip with the kids. It was a wonderful trip. We had to buy chains for the van, as there was a major snowstorm and we could not go through the pass without chains. David and I shared dinner while the kids enjoyed a TV show in the hotel room. It was in the midst of this romantic dinner that he announced to me, "we are going back to Bloomsburg."

I stared into his face in shock. We had committed to going to Oklahoma. We can't go back to Bloomsburg. I had emotionally and physically left Bloomsburg. I suddenly began to cry like I don't remember crying. "I can't go back. It is in the past."

I later realized that David had not left Bloomsburg emotionally and it was his lifeline. He had begun a long career of sending 4x6 photographs as postcards to friends and family. He had maintained his Bloomsburg persona. It took more than six months for me to return to myself in Bloomsburg and find my new life there.

David …
Our two years on the Navajo reservation came to an end. I had begun my stint as a Major, and was leaving as a Lt. Colonel. Not too bad. It had been an interesting learning experience, but we were ready to go. We packed up and headed back to Bloomsburg, taking our horses with us.

Left: David on Matressa

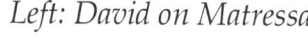

Below: Ready to go RVing about 1979

Blair …

When we were leaving the reservation to travel back to Pennsylvania, the people of the clinic had a wonderful going away party for us. I had worked with the Native social worker Marie during the two years, sharing and learning many cultural traditions to help in our care of the people. On the last day of rounds before we were to leave, Marie told me she had a dream about me in the future. She saw many people gathered around me as I lay in a bed. She described the house she saw me living in when so ill. I stopped her before she told me what she saw happen to me.

That last night I was on call, and a young woman came in with a fulminant pneumonia. She died, and we suspected she had tuberculosis, but it was not confirmed. The final diagnosis was never confirmed, though years later a critical illness, Hanta virus, was discovered on the reservation. That young woman may have died of that infection. For months after leaving Crownpoint I was preoccupied with the thought that I acquired whatever that woman had the last night I was on call. However, no serious illness ever occurred and Marie never responded to my cards and calls to follow up with her friendship. I finally concluded she was, in her dream, saying a final good bye to me.

Chapter 12
Return to Bloomsburg

DAVID...

We were preparing to leave the reservation the summer of 1983. I asked our friend Bill to haul the horse trailer and horses back to Pennsylvania for us.

Bill is an old cowboy who has been a good friend over the years, and still is today. We met him on the reservation, and he taught our kids how to ride. He's had an interesting life that included several marriages, and lots of kids, one of whom is a daughter he has never seen. He was sixteen when he got a girlfriend pregnant and took off from New York to the wild west. He married another woman, got her pregnant, and went to Korea. That marriage failed. He married again, this time having six kids, but found out the last two weren't his when he caught his wife in bed with his partner. That ended, and he married again. There were no kids from this one, but his wife's father and brothers moved in with them, and Bill was the only one working. That marriage ended after a year.

When we met him, he was living with a girl on the reservation, and he said that was his only illicit relationship. While he was with her, the ex-wife came down and took all his stuff: horse, saddle, rifle, everything. He eventually was able to retrieve his saddle and rifle, but the girlfriend wasn't happy about all the ruckus, and kicked him out.

He was down in the dumps, with no place to live, and wanted to go back east to see his sick mother. I gave him $500 and a Kachina doll, and sent him on his way. Blair said that would be the last I'd see of my $500. Three months later he came back, with my $500 and a new wife. We've been great friends ever since.

So while Bill was hauling the horses to his place in New York—where they'd stay until we returned—the family was packing up in preparation for leaving the reservation. We left in July 1983, and drove back east, looking forward to a more normal lifestyle.

Back home in Pennsylvania, we bought a beautiful stone house on six acres in Orangeville, with a long road leading

up to the house. Cowboy Bill and his brother built a six-stall stable for the four horses. We kept grain and hay in the extra two stalls. The horses were free to go in and out, but preferred to be outside. They'd only go in the stall to poop, and then amble back out, so I just closed them out to save myself the hassle of cleaning.

In addition to the horses, we raised a wide variety of animals. I never had pets as a child, but I believe if you want to learn about something, get involved in it. If you want to learn about animals, get something to raise. If you want to learn about stocks, buy one and follow it.

The kids always had dogs, cats and birds as pets, and we also had a lamb that we fed with outdated baby formula from the practice. It grew up thinking it was a dog, and ran in and out of the house with the dogs. When Lambchop got close to 100lbs. we had to say good bye and gave her to friends who had a farm. I bought chicken, geese and duck eggs and raised them after they hatched, along with rabbits, guinea hens and turkeys.

We raised the poultry and rabbits for the meat, but I could never kill anything, so I'd have someone else handle the butchering and cleaning. The rabbit guy would take the pelts and bring the meat back to us. We kept one male and one female of the ducks and geese, and took the others to a friend to kill and smoke the meat for us. Some of the turkeys were so big that the oven once caught fire from all the grease spilling over the pan.

By 1984 we had settled into our new home and back into our practice. Not ones to keep the status quo for long, we discussed having another child. We would have liked to adopt one from the reservation while we were there, but the Indians considered that "stealing" and we knew it wasn't a possibility.

Blair had been thinking about going to grad school and getting a Master's degree in Public Health. She debated whether to do that or have another baby. I said "Why spend money to go to grad school so you can make $80,000 a year, when you're earning $150,000 now. Just adopt another baby!"

We met with our friend Lois from the adoption agency and told her we were ready to adopt again, and that we wanted older children. We completed all the paperwork, and were almost finished with the six-week adoption class, when we were told of two children available right away. A 14-year-old girl and her 11-year-old brother were going to be split up because they were too old to go together to a new foster care home. They had already been in foster care five years. We only wanted one child, a boy, but Lois persuaded us to take them for the weekend to see how it went. We loved them both, and started the process, now having to pay double the adoption expense.

Celestia was a survivor, having spent five years in the foster care system. Charles acts today as though his life began with us, and that he has no prior history. He has never talked to anyone—even his wife—about his previous life.

Their mother had resisted giving up the kids, but finally agreed to relinquish her rights after meeting us. Celestia tried for a while to maintain communication with her mom, but it became too stressful. Charles, we believe, operates as if there was never any family but us.

Having five kids in the house was not always easy; especially since they were not only very close in age, but in or nearing their teen years. The two boys didn't get along with each other, and neither did the three girls. There wasn't much of a relationship until they were older and we went away for a weekend, leaving them under the watchful eye of Blair's father. He wasn't as diligent as he might have been, and the kids decided to have a party.

We always kept the liquor cabinet locked, but they weren't deterred. They turned it around, unscrewed the back, and helped themselves, watering down the bottles before returning them to the cabinet. The subterfuge bonded them together against us, and they began to have more rapport with each other. They became protective of one another, and to this day have not told whose idea it was to hit the liquor cabinet.

Matt has always been very laid back and easy going, and he loves his father. The first time he came to visit us after college, he went to a tattoo parlor and had Revak tattooed on his chest. He would never allow me to talk about his birth family. He'd say "I have no other family. You're my family."

His heritage is Puerto Rican, and Blairanne would get him books about the country and the culture, but he was never interested. However, he would later name his dog Diego.

One of our biggest mistakes as parents was not sticking to our guns when we came back from the reservation. We knew the education they received on the reservation was not up to par with the Pennsylvania school system, and we didn't want to set them up for failure, so we asked that our kids be held back a year. The teachers argued against it, saying "They'll be fine." So even though we knew the kids weren't performing at their grade level, we thought, "Well, the educators know best," and relented. But the teachers didn't know best, and the kids were soon struggling to keep up. I wished again that we had home-schooled them, either on the reservation or during their first year back home.

At the end of the year we transferred them to a private Catholic school, where Matt learned to drink. That school closed down, and we put him in another one where he learned to use drugs. We didn't know about the drugs until he was in rehab for alcohol abuse. By the time he was a freshman in college, he was heavy into both. When he wrecked his car that year and almost died, he told the police, "Call my parents. I need to do something, I have a problem."

The cops called and said, "Come down here, your son needs to talk to you."

I wrote a check for about $22,000 for a month of detox, and it worked.

As I look back, it doesn't seem that he was really addicted, like an alcoholic. He drinks socially now with no problem, and is extremely responsible, having held a great job for the last seventeen years. It seemed more like he was using alcohol to escape the friction among his siblings. He's a people-pleaser. We've often told him he should have been an only child, because he's normally calm and easy-going.

Our children are all very different, but seem to get along. Matt and Charles talk often, while Heather and Celestia manage a polite relationship. Shally is still the peacemaker and keeps everyone together.

In the 1970s, before we went to the reservation, I was moping around the house, and Blair told me I needed to get a hobby. Looking back, I wonder when I had time to mope, but it must have been a calm period of my life. So I took up stamp collecting, but working with small stamps often gave me a headache. We were living in the old mansion, and I was out digging post holes one day when I came across an Indian head penny from 1869. I thought this was pretty exciting, and I took it to Good as Gold numismatic shop, just a few blocks from where we lived downtown. I went in and asked what it was worth. The owner, Bob, said, "Well, about a dollar and a half. It's pitted, but in pretty good shape."

It had been in the ground for maybe a hundred years or more. We talked about coin collecting, and I told him I wanted a new hobby, so he gave me a jar of pennies and told me to take them home, look through them, and pick out what I wanted. He was a very trusting person.

I took the jar home and went through it for a couple of days. I picked out some pennies and took the jar back to him. I know now that I should have bought the whole jar full. Then he gave me a jar of buffalo nickels to go through, and I picked out a few of those.

The really valuable earlier dates weren't in there, but there were some good ones, and I ended up putting together about five nickel books. I had the three-legged buffalo, which sells for about $1500 bucks. Then I went to dimes, quarters, half-dollars and silver dollars.

I wish now that I'd kept them all, but I sold a lot of my collection before moving to Arizona, because they weighed a ton, and I was afraid they would be stolen. I sold them for about three times what I had paid, but now they're worth about six times that. I had three 1893-S silver dollars, and the cheapest one now is worth about $3600, and that's in bad shape! A good one would be about $12,000.

I doubled my money, selling them all for about ten grand. But now, the one I sold for $3800 is worth about twelve thousand, just 12 or 14 years later. I still have a lot of silver dollars, but not the ones that are really rare.

I have a lot of the large pennies, including two of the 1794 penny, which are worth about twelve or fourteen hundred each. The 1793 is worth about $12,000 now. I saw one of those, but never owned one. The large pennies weren't worth much back then: they'd go for about a buck apiece. I should've bought thousands of them. Now you can't touch them for under $20 apiece. They're rare, although no one knows how many are left. People would commonly use them as washers. I had a very rare 1803 penny in a collection, and sold that one coin for what the complete set had cost me.

Bob and I were going through some coins when I came across one I thought looked like an 1887 New Jersey copper. It had a ploughshare on one side and a horse head on the other. Bob said, "It might be, how much will you give me?"

"I'll give you $10 bucks for it."

Now it's worth a couple thousand dollars. That was back in the 1970s. A 2011 Heritage magazine has it going on auction soon, with a starting bid of 1,000 dollars.

The first coin in the United States was the 1792 dime. In 1793 a large penny was introduced, and the following year the first silver dollar was minted. One of those dollars, in the worst condition, would be worth twenty to thirty thousand dollars now. And one in mint condition recently sold for almost eight million dollars.

One day a guy came in to the shop while I was there, with a sheet of stamps that was printed upside down. Bob said "Let's buy it." We debated back and forth for a while, and the guy finally left. Now just one of those stamps is worth twenty to thirty thousand dollars. I wish we'd bought them all. I definitely made some mistakes along the way.

Experts always say to get a collection that is worth something; that will go up in value. That's why I got interested in coins, antiques, paintings, art, stamps, and so on. I used to buy all those sheets of stamps. In the 1980s, I could still buy sheets of stamps from the 1930s, and '40s. Bob would sell me a sheet of 100 three-cent stamps for $2.50. I must have bought thousands of dollars' worth of stamps.

Years later, when Bob was going out of business, I went in to the shop one day and asked how much he wanted for all the sheets of stamps. He gave me a good price, so I bought them all. He said "I'll make money no matter what I charge you," so we were both happy.

These uncirculated stamps from the 1910s, '20s and '30s, have been sitting in a box for the last ten or fifteen years, so there might be some good ones in there.

Bob was a good guy, and as honest as the day is long. I did a lot of dealing with him over the years, and we became very good friends.

David & Blair

CHAPTER 13
Celestia

*"If You Pull His Finger,
There is Always a Gas Explosion"*

BLAIR ...

Men notoriously enjoy the exchange and sharing of stories and experiences of farting. It seems to pervade man caves and the spots that men gather, BUT, this man never needed a cave or an all-male audience. David loved to change the scenery, change the tenor of the talk and most importantly loved to fart. I am certain there are enough stories to create our own "David farts" book.

Golf was never part of our lifestyle. In fact, I deliberately avoided golf as it was seen by many as "what doctors do". David always complained it took a whole day. And anything that allowed a man to be separated from his wife, including long distance running, biking and especially golf, David called family-and-marriage-avoiders. So he only played golf when he had an opportunity to help with a benefit. His clubs were from the Salvation Army and had some experience driving stones out of the driveway.

The team he joined had an avid younger man. Just as Joe swung to hit the ball, David farted. That messed up Joe's shot and created such anger he swung and broke his driver on the ground. David laughed momentarily only, but enjoyed sharing that story for years.

My favorite story with the explosive outcomings of David was the subject of a humorous speech I gave at Toastmasters. We are in Italy, cramped with bags that have to be taken to the 8th floor on a small 4-by-6-foot elevator. Tony and David load on some of those bags and are joined by a local woman heading to the 3rd floor. As the woman leaves the elevator on the 3rd floor and the door closes to move the two of them upward, David announces to Tony, "that is one lucky woman". Tony turns to ask the reason for that woman's luck, just as David lets fly one large, odiferous fart. Choking with the contaminated air in a closed space, Tony grabs David's neck, trying to seek revenge, as David roars with laughter. Never practice an elevator speech with David, was the learned rule.

Amaya was barely three years old when she delighted in pulling Poppy's finger for the announcing gas. When David had died and we had a family meal five short months later, I asked the kids to share a special story they liked about Poppy. Amaya jumped up to announce that she liked to pull Poppy's finger.

Celestia grew to enjoy Dad's unique behaviors but it came slowly, as she had a major adjustment to make in joining this crazy, very openly operating family. Having lived in foster care for five years, she had adjusted to routine and an organized, controlled life. Our social worker, Lois, announced when she wanted to introduce Charles and Celestia to us, "they look healthy, I see survivors when I look into her and Charles' eyes."

A one-day visit introduced our family to the potential new sister and brother. A later weekend visit firmed our response when Lois said, "Children's services will have to split them up to find a new foster home. It is hard to place two older kids in one home. And if you take them, we will seek the mothers' voluntary relinquishment of her rights. She has consented to that if she can meet you. And they will be yours."

Dramatic lifestyle changes were certainly ahead for all of us. We had barely returned from the two-year stint on the Navajo Reservation and now we were expanding our family.

I was considering going to graduate school to earn a masters degree in Public Health, but the alternative plan to enlarge the family came easily. David had not been happy with my thought of grad school. "Pay for school and earn less than you can as a physician? That is crazy," he said.

He voted for the family expansion. I voted for the family expansion. And though somewhat reluctant,

Heather, Matthew and Shally voted for the family expansion. And we did!

The law had just changed in Pennsylvania, so the time in our care for formal adoption was six months. How quickly that time flew by. It was now five Revak kids.

You always hear those adoption stories of how the adopted child looks like the family? We now had four red-heads. No plan of our own. And interestingly, Celestia has often said how many times people have commented on how much she looked like her mother (me).

We visited their biological mother, who gave her consent to their adoption. A new adjustment was now possible for all of us. It went pretty smoothly, I would say. Each of the kids had their own bedroom. Celestia kept contact with her mother by letter. And over the years she maintained that contact, including one Easter holiday when she brought her mother to visit for the day.

I must insert here that I did not fret over the adoption process, and I did not fret over a fear that their mother would try to take Celestia and Charles from us. I felt completely confident that they were our kids. (I tell in Matthew's story of the occasion I thought I met a potential mother for him and became absolutely panic stricken; obviously we did not know his mother.)

Celestia is a bright lady; she did well in school, usually out-scoring Heather in report card performance. Though they were the same age and in the same grade, there was not a sisterly acknowledgement for either of them. And all social activities became independent for each of them.

Parties happened at the house of my adolescent kids: two 15-year-old boys and two 17-year-old girls drew a great gathering one weekend when David and I slipped away for a break. My Dad was to be keeping an eye on them. We later learned the key on the liquor cabinet was not necessary for its entry when you had creative kids figuring out how to remove the back side slats when the need for alcohol was expressed.

The knock at the door on Monday after our return, and the announcement that we could be arrested for contributing to the delinquency of minors when Eric did not return to his home, was announced to us by his dad. That announcement prompted my visit to the skating rink and to friends houses to gather the Revak violators and bring them home to a family meeting. We can share with you that that was probably the solidifying family event. The four kids acknowledged the act, no one confessed and no one blamed the other, as they "stuck together" in their defense of the firmly announced punishments. We don't know of other "teenage libations" at our house. There were more experiences they all shared, but all seemed to occur off Revak territory.

Heather shared only recently the escape through a cottage bathroom window, which she accomplished with friends when the police arrived to investigate. As recently as 2013 we have heard of other adolescent capers. No police holdings occurred that we know of.

Celestia began work as a busgirl at the Inn at Turkey Hill when she started her freshman year at Bloomsburg University. She quickly attached a romance of sorts with Tim, the chef. When a truck arrived and we discovered she was moving her bedroom furniture out of her room, she shared that she was leaving because she was pregnant.

That experience prompted the closure of her college career for many long years. With a mixture of pregnancies and work, she eventually achieved that Bachelor's degree online from Kaplan College.

Sabrina was born in 1988 and Celestia continued her independent living. She soon separated from the relationship with Tim and several years later met and married David. Soon after, in 1996, Larissa was born, and then David in 2002.

A fiery independence and that "survivor" eye that Lois, our adoption manager saw, showed itself in a wonderfully accomplished mother of three children. After David and I lived in a mobile home one year while we were building a house, David offered the home to Celestia and was terribly disappointed when she refused. This is a mother who never boasted or decried her single motherhood status. This is a mother who gave time and every talent she had to these three kids. This is a mother who coached and still coaches soccer, and who sought and found male figures to step in for her son. This is a lady who patiently waited and carefully protected her kids when their estranged father did not pay or show up for special occasions, whether holidays or financial obligations. Celestia works in a private insurance office and devotes her love to her three kids.

At this writing, Sabrina has just purchased a house with husband Warren and they continue to share parenting of Warren's son Logan with Logan's mother. (An update: In January 2016 Warren and Sabrina obtained full custody of Logan). Larissa is starting her college sophomore year with a transfer from Susquehanna University to Bloomsburg University. She will live at home and work part time. And David is starting the year playing in the band, and continuing soccer and wrestling. When asked something special he remembers about Poppy, David wrote to me how Poppy would always say to him, "Let's go drain our lizards." Celestia got an advisory call from his teacher in 3rd grade when David announced his need to do that in the midst of class.

Celestia remained married to Dave even when she knew there were issues she didn't want to deal with. His erratic drinking, his unreliable service as a truck driver, and his irresponsible behavior resulted in many issues, I am certain. There never were distressing or disturbing reports given to us about Dave. Every attempt was made to walk Dave through "growing up" and fathering his children.

And to this day there have been friends and special relationships for Celestia, but no commitment to a partnership that I am aware of.

I must say that our move from the East to Arizona in 2001 made our long-distance relationship pretty thin with Celestia, Matthew and Charles.

In March 2015, Matthew and Jenny, with four-year-old Madelyn, crossed the country to make the Revak family more western than eastern. David always asked and encouraged the kids to move west. He and I so enjoyed their shared lives and looked forward to watching the grandkids grow with our arms around them.

Could or would Celestia pull Dad's finger? He adored her, but she stood her independence. I remember after one year of our adoption adjustment, feeling David's grief at not having the relationship he sought with this new daughter. A visit to our adoption case manager, Lois, reaffirmed our knowledge that 14 years of growth and foster care did not prepare Celestia for a close-knit father-daughter relationship. But over the years she has demonstrated and shared a lot of her mature mother/daughter/father strengths in her role as daughter.

Warren, Sabrina, Blair, David, Celestia, Larissa and Charles

Below: Sabrina with Logan & Warren

Chapter 14
Charles

"I Get Better Looking Every Day"

BLAIR ...
If a mirror was in sight we were honored to hear the much-shared quote, "Why do you think I do that?" or "What do you think of that photo of me? You see, <u>I get better looking every day</u>"

And believe me, a mirror was not a required prop; we often heard that quote without a reflection necessary and without our questioning it.

I also am reminded that when we first started dating, David would often tell me that people thought he looked like the actor Paul Newman. I, who never attended movies, often wondered why he reminded me of his handsome self-copy. And why Paul Newman, I never knew. I was thinking he may have been in David's favorite movie, Shane, but that was Alan Ladd and Jack Palance. So that didn't work. Paul Newman was a handsome actor.

I think Charles chose to share this statement of David's as it spoke of an eccentricity of his dad that made no sense. What did it have to do with anything? It did have the power to create laughter and warm communion wherever David found himself. And it supported his commitment to always be on stage. His ever-announced comment about his day was, "It's showtime." It is only one of many comments Charles garnered from a life with Dad/Doc/David as he called him.

May I first comment on Charles? And may I say over and over again what a dynamic of love and relationship one could find with him. Charles wrote a poem about his dad when he was in college. And when he brought a birthday gift wrapped in handmade paper, with all of the quotations one could have remembered said by his dad, David was overwhelmed. He repeated out loud, "He was listening to me, I never thought he was."

It was the occasion of David's 65th birthday. I had planned a weekend in Las Vegas with the whole family. And to our surprise, the girls told my brother Mike and his wife Peg about it. So Mike and Peg and Michelle came also for the birthday. We stayed at the Excalibur, I think. We had dinner in the Renaissance restaurant where we saw the fighting and ate our chicken legs with our bare hands. It was a wonderful family celebration. It would be the only time we celebrated together as a family until the celebration of life after David's death.

Charles came to us at the age of 11 years. He and Celestia had been in foster care for five years. He had a fair complexion, strawberry-red hair and a look that sometimes swirled with implosive and nearly explosive fear or anger and created an uncertainty for nearly a year.

On one occasion that look appeared in a disciplinary situation. Charles had pushed someone in the pool at the Gaynor's house and he was instructed not to do that. A look on his face and in his eyes created for us a questioning and fearful sense. That look smoldered momentarily, but never burst forth. And soon it was gone forever. What did it mean? We shall never know.

The first week Charles and Celestia were with us, the boys were sent to shovel the manure out of the horse stalls. Shortly after they should have been done, David went to check on the job. Charles, flushed with sneezing and wheezing, greeted Dad wielding a pitchfork full of hay and manure. "Why didn't you tell me you were allergic to hay?" was David's question. Charles responded, "I don't know." Cleaning the stalls was no longer a Charles job.

To survive the life of five kids I found color-coded socks and household duty charts helpful.

Life had no past history for Charles. Celestia carried, folded in an album, a handfull of photos. One she said was Charles as a baby. There was no identifying information, other than it was a baby Charles photo. It gave us the only history we had. One other photo had the two of them on a porch step. Celestia refused to part with those photos, holding them close to her.

Near the time of Charles' marriage to Denise, Celestia brought forward the photos, but not to be handled by anyone other than herself. I later got permission to copy the photo of Charles as a baby. Charles did not know any history associated with that photo and, as far as he was concerned, there was no history. On a few occasions, I pressed him for answers. "That half-brother we heard about; do you remember anything about him?"

"No," Denise commented, "his life began when he came to you."

Indeed, it appeared there was no life before Charles became our son. To this day, as a 42-year-old, there is never offered any information about a life before his life with us.

That life with us grew into a wonderful connected life of love. We sensed Charles and Celestia shared no more history before their life with us than they did after that life began with us. They shared very little connection with each other.

His life developed into a man with a wonderful sense of humor and love. It was a sense of humor that mounted to Dad's competition. As Charles advanced through high school and then college at Lock Haven, he joined and found great connection with the fraternity. David never let me enter the frat house when we visited or picked up Charles at school. He assured me I didn't want to see the type of lifestyle going on there.

And Charles did appear to not only connect, but to get into over-exuberant college fraternity life. When his grades threatened probation we stopped payment on school assuming he would move home. Instead he sought and acquired a loan to cover his college expenses and brought his GPA up to a glowing range. At graduation, David paid off the loan and Charles soon moved to full time work. He graduated with a degree in Recreation Therapy and became a counsellor with an upward bound program that cared for boys with adolescent bad behavior. Though he talked little about those experiences, we were convinced he grew and gained much maturity and understanding working with the director of the program and the boys.

As adolescent teenage boys, Charles and Matthew did some things together. Both have shy personalities. After many years, we learned about those drop-offs at the movie theater; David took them to the door and watched them enter so we knew where they were. What we didn't know was they were timed for a run out the side door of the theater to an open fraternity party up the street. They always timed their visits well, so that the post theater pick up was on time.

I so remember the time I was late picking the boys up after a soccer match. I did forget. But using my creative parenting, I proceeded to tell them waiting had benefits. We learn how to cope with issues while waiting, we can be creative with our time, we can even read and study our books while waiting. How fortunate these boys were to have my insights. Only days later as I arrived home to find the door locked, I frowned impatiently as Charles ambled, hesitated and rested until he let me in. And as the door finally opened to my demands, my Charles commented, "It is good to wait."

Repetition is the mother of learning. We talked about this with Heather's story but will repeat it, as "Repetition is the mother of learning." So often, a mis-practice of adolescence resulted in a fatherly discussion. And it wasn't without repetition that those meetings occurred, especially with Matthew and Charles. You know the consequences of that behavior, you know how that can influence your future opportunities and choices. And their response would always be,"but Dad, we heard that lecture before."

"Yes, and you need to hear it again, you know repetition is the mother of learning. My mother would tell me that when I misbehaved."

And so the discipline became filled with the anticipated, "Yes, we know Dad; 'repetition is the mother of learning.'"

And don't you know, no matter how angry you can be at your kids, and how upset, embarrassed, disappointed you can be in their behavior, it is a winning strategy when a smile, even a laugh can lighten—but never erase—the importance of parental discipline.

Charles had completed his degree in Recreation therapy and worked several jobs helping kids who were off track in their lives. He soon shared his observation that though he loved the work, the money would never be a good living. He had always been interested in, and worked and played many hours on the computer. He learned of the new Master's degree program at Bloomsburg University and decided to apply to the program. David happened to have a conversation with the director of the program in the dentist's waiting room soon after Charles applied.

Henry asked if Charles was related to him. David replied yes and proceeded to campaign for Charles' opportunity in the program. He was accepted and excelled. That led him to a good career in Instructional technology. He began his career with a refrigeration corporation, worked for several defense industry companies and now helps companies establish Human Resources programs through his program building. While a student at Bloomsburg, Charles met Denise, who owned and managed her own beauty salon in Bloomsburg. Not long afterward we were called from Las Vegas where they had escaped to bind the wedding love relationship. We celebrated at our house with a Blessing of the wedding and reception after they came home. Denise has a wonderful enthusiasm and a great giving spirit. She has moved from her own salon to other related careers and most recently has started a program to be a nurse. She relates childhood dreams of that career.

Soon after their marriage, the decision came to widen the family. Two boys, Jaiden who is now 8, and Jude, who is 6, have bounced the family into lively, high-charged living. Recently Jaiden fractured his arm. Having watched the two of them jumping, and scrambling in trees and diving into furniture with flips, it was a surprise so me that the first occasion waited so long.

Charles not only made the collection of quotations of Dad/Doc/David, he also composed a poem about him. It was so very special and rich that he volunteered to read that poem at the celebration of life service for David in Bloomsburg. The humor and love of his family and the rich strength of Charles relay so much of the richness of David, and Charles' life with David. When she calls me, Denise often tells of a funny quote Charles shares from his dad. Most recently they were ready to eat dinner and he announced to the boys, "Flap-a-Lip," a favorite Dad-ism.

Ode to Pappa Bear Revak

There once was a man from Mt. Carmel
Never to be labeled as normal

He would walk in the room with a grin on his chin
Boasting of his new soup that someday would make him quite thin

You may have heard the great stories of the babies he did deliver
Be wary of the request to pull a finger, the stench could make you shiver

There are lectures on money, politics, education, and vicissitudes too
But never take a glance if you hear, "like my new shoes"

Pictures come in the mail like a story from a past letter
Reminding us all that our correspondence could be better

He lives and explores, hand and hand with his dove
The guidance he gave was full of his love

Experiences were shared, some good and some bad
But the luckiest of us all were able to call him our dad.

Love, Charles

Charles with Jude, Jaiden & Denise

Chapter 15
Yeah, It's Cancer

DAVID ...

"Yeah, it's cancer. See you Tuesday."

It was the spring of 1991, and we were still living in Orangeville. Blairanne and I had just returned from Mexico, where we had been chaperoning a group of kids with our daughter Shally's high school class. Some of the group had gone to a party, and when they still hadn't returned by midnight, Blair became worried and insisted that we go look for them. As we walked the streets, going up and down hills, my breathing became more labored.

I had been aware of my decreasing energy levels during the last couple of months. I was tired all the time, and experienced shortness of breath just walking around our large yard or playing with the animals. I didn't feel well, but couldn't pinpoint anything in particular. It seemed like just a simple case of fatigue, but it hung around for too long. In the past, I had done some jogging when I had time, and it never bothered me; but now, just walking up a flight of stairs was exhausting.

Before the Mexico trip, I talked to our family doctor about my lethargy, and had mentioned it to other doctor friends, but they would just say, "You're overworked" or "You're probably just depressed."

I insisted that nothing had changed in my life. Everything was as it had been for years. I wasn't working any harder than I always had, and I had no reason to be depressed.

Now, in Mexico, the tiredness and labored breathing were becoming more evident. I decided that as soon as we were home, I would have a complete checkup and find out once and for all what was wrong.

We had barely unpacked when I discovered the lump in my neck. I made an appointment to see an Ear, Nose, Throat doctor at the Geisinger Medical Center. He did a thorough checkup and also felt the lump.

He said, "You're a doctor, what do you think it is?"

I was in denial, and half-jokingly, said, "I think it's a tuberculosis nodule, just scrofula or something."

He said, "No, it's cancer," and then walked out of the room and left us sitting there to absorb that.

We waited while a biopsy was done. Then the doctor stuck his head in the door and said, "Yeah, it's cancer. See you Tuesday."

Those words, tossed out so nonchalantly, would affect the next two years of my life, and bring up a lot of unresolved conflict.

"You have cancer" are three of the most dreaded words you will ever hear.

Even though I was a physician, I reacted pretty much the way anyone else would. I had resisted having tests done until Blair finally convinced me to do so in late June. I was in denial ... and I just didn't want to be sick. I didn't have time for a serious illness.

I knew I'd have to deal with it sooner or later, and so finally gave in. It was determined to be Hodgkins lymphoma. Once again I handled it just like anyone else would; with anger and frustration. By this time, Blair was more in denial than I was.

Blair ...
The announcement of the cancer shot through our lives with a major blow. I was just elected President of the Medical Staff of the Bloomsburg Hospital. That was always known to be a major time commitment for any physician, let alone one who is losing the busiest practicing physician in the practice to chemotherapy and radiation therapy. I remember vividly, while walking for exercise, agonizing, talking to God and questioning why, and how would I handle this. Suddenly, a breath came over me saying, "this is a hoax, he doesn't really have cancer."

Now there was a lifting feeling; a feeling that I could make it through all of this. I certainly knew that we were dealing with the reality of cancer. Now I could do it. But within weeks David had me struggling with the survival and how we were going to manage issues. He went to the bike shop in town and purchased a bicycle. He needed to be assured it was a good, long-lasting bike and he paid $800.00 for it.

Just before the treatment started he flew to Utah to visit Bill and ride horses. There Matressa chose him, and out of the pack of horses she nestled up to David. David negotiated with the rancher and bought the horse. After the first chemo treatment, he waited to greet me at the door, modeling his brand new tuxedo. "I may need this, and besides, you can always put it on me to bury me".

My responses could not have been more overwhelming. "You are struggling with a deadly disease, you are not working, so the income is down dramatically, and you buy a bike, a horse and a tuxedo?"

There he was, speaking of his plan to live through this, and he did.

David ...
Lymph nodes are tissues located throughout the body that act as a filter to fight infections. The cancerous cells spread to various organs and, if untreated, eventually kill the patient.

Statistically, my chances of living another five years were only about sixty percent, but I had faith that I would beat those odds.

I had seen in my patients the benefits of having a positive outlook during recovery, and was determined to maintain a positive mental attitude myself. I also knew that keeping my sense of humor could only help.

It seemed to take forever for me to get a specific diagnosis and to stage the cancer. Staging is a way of measuring the progression of the cancer. In Stage One the cancer is in the neck; Stage Two it's in the chest; Stage Three, the abdomen; and by Stage Four it's in the bone and other organs. By then a bone marrow transplant is generally needed.

I went through an extended work up, which took almost three months. We knew the cancer was in my neck, but weren't sure if it had reached my chest and abdomen. Bone marrow testing was done, as well as an angiogram, which was an all-day procedure. I had the option of letting them cut me open to see what stage the cancer was in, or having them put dye in a drip and run it very slowly through my lymph system. I chose the drip. They found that the cancer had spread to the groin, stomach, chest and neck. The radiologists couldn't seem to agree, however, on whether or not it was actually in the abdomen. Five of them said it was, and another four said it was not. There wasn't an absolute decision as to whether it was in the abdomen or not.

These days, they do a non-invasive CAT scan, to see what's going on, but back then it was a little more complicated. After two different bone marrows, I was treated as Stage Three.

Blair wanted me to go to a specialist at New York's, Sloan-Kettering hospital to have someone else to look at it. But I refused, saying that I wanted to be treated as if it was below abdomen, to be sure.

In mid-August, I began chemotherapy treatments, which were given every two weeks for the next six to eight months. I had been seeing patients up until that point, but gave it up in early August. Even though I would have liked to continue seeing patients, by now it was not only more difficult, but it could have been dangerous. I was getting tired faster, and I knew the chemo was going to sap even more of my energy. I was also more susceptible to other diseases now that my immune system was weakened, and I couldn't afford to risk being around sick patients.

We had recently taken on a new associate—Jody Hutson—so I was able to turn many of my patients over to him. On August 14th, I saw my last patient, and made plans to go back to work the following April.

I was regularly getting the necessary treatment, followed by a CT scan. The doctor said it looked like the cancer wasn't going to respond to the treatment. Blair again suggested we go to New York, but I still wasn't ready.

The radiology lab was two or three stories underground, with the chemo department next to it. We had to go down a couple of floors, then walk through a tunnel into a darkened room with no windows. There were usually thirty or forty other patients—all of whom looked like hell. All the TV stations were tuned to soap operas. Overall, it was a depressing place to be.

I'd sit there in that already dreary, windowless room, and look around to see paintings with little plaques saying, "In memory of...," "Dedicated to...," and so on. It was extremely demoralizing. I said to the receptionist, "What kind of place are you running here? You're sending these people a message that they're going die!"

Doctors would often say to me, "You've got one of the 'better' cancers." I just wanted to smack them when I heard that, because it didn't make any difference. I still had to suffer through the chemo and radiation, along with all the anxiety they produced.

The chemo treatment took about six to eight hours. They'd load me up with steroids, and then pump four different drugs into me. The steroids made me nuts: I was all puffed up, I'd hallucinate, and I couldn't eat or sleep. And they made me nervous for another reason. I was pretty sure I had the tuberculosis bacterium in my body from the years of taking care of my uncle Albert. Once you get the bacteria, you never get rid of it, but it's walled off, and usually doesn't do any damage. However, the steroids can break down those walls, allowing the TB to flare up. Just one more thing to worry about.

The treatment was almost worse than the disease. The radiation made my trachea and esophagus so sore that I couldn't swallow. I'd get so anxious about the chemotherapy that I felt like just jumping out of the chair. I was eventually given a Mediport; a line directly into the heart which allows the meds to be pumped throughout the body in about half the time. When you're sitting there going through the treatment, cutting back from a six-to-eight hour stint, to three or four hours, is a real blessing. Even so, I was weak, sick, frustrated, and I thought I was dying. Not a good place to be.

While I was going through the chemo, someone from the newspaper called me one day. "You're not working?" he asked.

I said, "No I can't, because I shouldn't be around people with my immune system so low. My white count is down to almost nothing, and if I get sick I could die."

The reporter asked if I would give an interview to talk about it, and I said, "Sure, I'm just home alone with my dog, and Blair is working all the time." I chatted with the reporter for a while, and he wrote a good article.

Shortly after it appeared in the paper, I received an interesting phone call from Leonard Majikas. He was a psychologist who worked for the State of Pennsylvania, in Wilkes-Barre doing drug and alcohol rehabilitation during the day. In the evenings, he practiced hypnotherapy in his own clinic. He provided sex therapy, trauma therapy, help for marital problems—whatever the patient needed—using post-hypnotic suggestion or tapes with the appropriate messages.

His office was very professional and comfortable, and consisted of several therapy rooms. I entered one of the rooms, and he had me sit in a plush recliner that massaged my back. He put a mask on my eyes, and gave me a set of earphones.

He explained that he could hypnotize me so that I could better tolerate the chemotherapy. I had mentioned in the article that it had caused me to be sick as a dog with nausea. He put me under, and then began telling me, "You will feel

Recovering with a smile

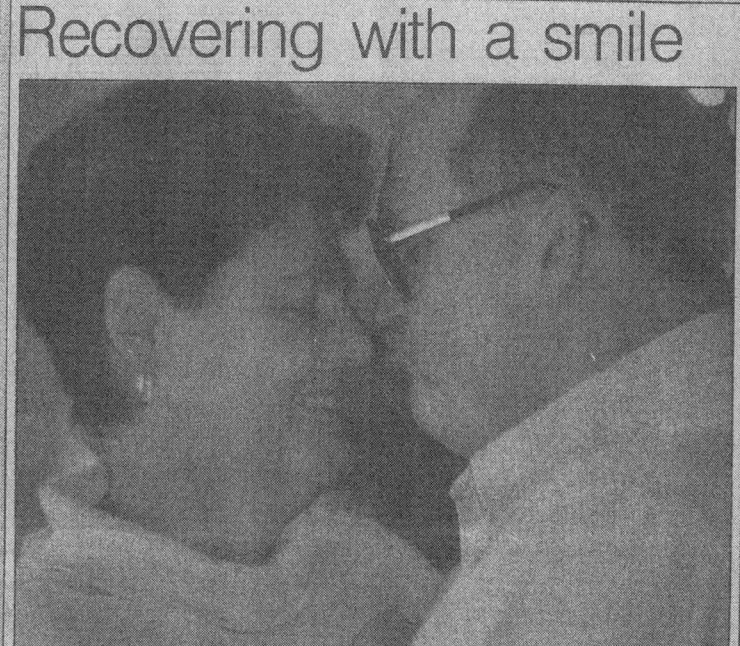

MAKE IT BETTER — Dr. David Revak jokingly gives his wife, Blair, a kiss on the nose at their Orangeville home Saturday. Revak is on the road to recovery from Hodgkin's lymphoma, a cancer of the lymph nodes.

Doctor's humor is his best medicine

By TERRIE MORGAN
Press-Enterprise staff

ORANGEVILLE — He has no feeling in his hands or feet and has lost some hair, but David Revak is happy this holiday season. He should be. He's winning.

He's winning the battle against Hodgkin's lymphoma, a cancer of the lymph nodes which for the past six months has forced the Bloomsburg physician to undergo extensive chemotherapy.

The never-ending nausea. The extreme fatigue. Drug after drug injected into his body. He's been through it all.

But David Revak still laughs. He tells jokes, often about his cancer. It's that attitude, he said, that's helped him into remission.

"In the concentration camps the ones who survived were the ones who had a sense of humor and a sense of caring," he said in an interview at his home Saturday. "People who are rigid don't survive. People who believe in numbers don't survive."

It was numbers that three weeks ago made the 51-year-old family practitioner and his wife, Blair, momentarily believe he had lost the fight.

Test results showed no change, meaning the chemotherapy had not worked. He had perhaps just months to live, they thought.

But it turned out that it was just a matter of interpretation. The doctor who normally sees him was away, so someone else interpreted the results.

Please see **RECOVERY** *back page*

That doctor was not as familiar with his case as his doctor who, upon his return, quickly assured the couple things had indeed changed. The lumps in his neck were smaller. He was getting better.

But even in that darkest moment when he believed all the pain and sickness had been for nothing, Revak's humor shone through.

"He was telling me when I do my Christmas shopping, buy him a gift that won't last more than six months," Blair said.

Despite the good news, David has not won yet. After one more session of chemotherapy, he starts six weeks of radiation treatments.

Then he waits to see if the cancer returns. If he remains free of cancer for five years, he will be considered cured.

In the meantime, David plans to return by July to the medical practice he's shared with his wife for 25 years.

> It's so tough on the spouse and I guess I have not been the greatest spouse. I try to understand that she has needs. She's working all kinds of hours and she's tired. When you're sick, you forget they need support too.
>
> **Dr. David Revak**
> *talking about his wife, Blair*

He's anxious to get back to work, to regain control of his life. And anxious, he said, to free his wife from the effects of his illness.

"It's so tough on the spouse and I guess I have not been the greatest spouse," he said. "I try to understand that she has needs. She's working all kinds of hours and she's tired. When you're sick, you forget they need support too."

"One thing that would happen was when I began to express my frustration with what was happening with his disease, he'd shut me down," Blair said. "That made me very angry."

Blair said she also felt frustrated and angry, but she wouldn't know why.

"I'd be very tense, irritable and impatient with him, then I realized it was because he was very anxious," she said. "As soon as his treatments were over, it would be gone."

But the couple said they were determined that David's illness affect their relationship as little as possible.

The most important thing was to remain genuine with one another, they said. If David did something that angered her, cancer or not, he was told about it.

"I came home one night and the sink was full of dishes, the counter was a mess. I was tired and I started yelling at him," Blair said. "He said 'I had such a busy day and besides, I have cancer,'" she said with a laugh.

They were real feelings from real people, an aspect of recovery the couple said is critical in keeping a marriage together.

"I think you have to live your existence like you've always lived. I don't think you put your relationship on hold and live a false existence," Blair said.

That's why they agreed to share their story once again, as they had five months ago shortly after David was diagnosed.

They want others to know that it's tough, but you can make it through. David Revak has. And he's done it with a smile.

good and very strong after your next chemo session. You will have to pee first, and you will pee all the cancer out of your system."

He described chemo as being like the little PacMan critters that would go through my body chomping at the cancer cells, which would then be eliminated through my urine. Then he said, "You'll be very hungry afterward."

I thought that was great, because I usually had no appetite after chemo. The hypnotherapy itself was wonderful! When I came out from it, he said, "Tonight you're going to sleep very soundly and get a good night's rest."

I went home, went to bed and slept just great. Better yet, the next time I had a treatment, it worked exactly as he said it would. I was able to go out to breakfast, eat hearty, and feel fine afterward.

I tried to pay him, but he refused to take my money, saying, "Don't you remember what you did for me? Twenty years ago, I was in graduate school, and went to see you when I was sick. You could tell I had other things on my mind as well, and asked what was wrong. I told you I had wanted to take my kids to Disneyland, but we weren't able to go. You asked where I lived, and the next thing I knew, you were driving up to my house in your motorhome and told me to use it for the trip to Disneyland."

He said, "It was a very generous gesture, because we couldn't have gone anywhere without that. And now you want me to charge you?"

Ed Christine

Dr. Dave, alive and joking

BLOOMSBURG — Dave Revak knows it's coming. Any day now. Maybe even today.

It always comes this time of the year. Just like clockwork. Why should this one be any different?

"They're gonna ask me to be in the Bloom'n Follies again," Revak said. "I'll do it. I always do.

"But why do you suppose they always ask me to dress in drag?"

Then he laughs. A big laugh. A laugh as natural as most people taking a gulp of air.

Chances are they ask because they know he'll do it. He always does.

Dave Revak is one of those guys who never met a joke he didn't like. Or a joke he didn't like to tell, or pull, or be part of.

Wigs, hats, fake noses, noisemakers. He has them all, somewhere. He can do Groucho and Donald Duck. He'll turn a napkin into Mickey Mouse ears . . . in a restaurant . . . with his daughter sitting there getting red.

The man has worn out whoopie cushions. No problem there, he has a backup. The old hand under the armpit trick still works.

A real cutup, that's what they all say about Dr. Dave over at Bloomsburg Hospital.

Remember the time he did his rounds on roller skates? Everybody loved it.

Maybe laughter isn't the best medicine but Dave Revak puts a lot of stock in its therapeutic value.

Except for that time last year when somebody asked about the lumps in his neck. That wasn't so

"So I worked at being a survivor."

Check this family doctor's background. He has delivered almost 3,000 babies, operated on people, injected people, written who knows how many prescriptions.

Traditional? Read on.

He also spent two years on an Indian reservation and still marvels at something he once saw a medicine man do. He has sent patients to chiropractors, suggested they see faith healers, clergymen, accupuncturists. He's been to the Hot Springs in Arkansas and recommends it highly.

Nobody should've been surprised when part of his therapy included sessions with a psychoanalyst. Before each chemotherapy treatment he had himself hypnotized.

"This doctor had me convinced I could feel the drugs eating up the cancer cells like Pac-Man," Revak said. "He also told me that 30 minutes into the session I would have this painful urge to urinate. Twenty-nine minutes later, I'd be running for the bathroom carrying an IV full of drugs."

Make a case that was supposed to be symbolic — a cleansing of the system. Yet, isn't there the slightest feeling that just maybe somebody was playing a joke on Dr. Dave this time?

There was also the day Revak and another guy got tired sitting around. They maxed their dosages and headed for Barbados.

"Don't ask me why," Revak joked. "We were all puffy from steroids, we couldn't go out in the sun, we couldn't drink. But it seemed like the thing to do."

I had forgotten all about the incident, but it goes to show that good deeds are often returned when we least expect it.

I had the opportunity to meet Dr. Bernie Siegel, a surgeon who routinely operated on cancer patients. He often noticed that some people who—medically—should have died, didn't; while others who probably shouldn't have succumbed to their illness … did. After much research, he found that prayer and belief in getting better did make a difference. Our minds control our health much more than we realize. He then wrote a book entitled, "Love, Medicine and Miracles," which was published in 1986.

There's a story about a woman in the hospital who was dying. But she kept insisting, "My granddaughter is getting married soon, and I've got to go to her wedding."

Though it was against the odds, she was still alive when the wedding took place, and was able to attend. The following Monday, a nurse went into her room and asked how the wedding was. They talked for a while, and as the nurse was was leaving, the old woman grabbed her hand and said, "I've got two more granddaughters."

I read Dr. Siegel's book, and realized I had much more power over my own recovery than I had believed, and I set about to do everything I could to continually get better. I've always had a healthy sense of humor, and used that to my advantage. Laughter has also been proven to be a benefit and boon to recovery, and in spite of the disease, I found plenty to laugh about.

I had read that in concentration camps; those who survived were often the ones who had a sense of humor. Depressed, rigid, negative people don't survive, nor do those who rely on data, statistics and numbers. All of those can be wrong, as I discovered.

In early December, my test results showed that there was no change in my condition. The chemo had not worked. The prognosis now would be that I might only have months to live. Then my regular doctor—who had been out of town—returned and looked at the results. He told us that the lumps were actually getting smaller, the chemo was working, and I was making progress. The first person to read the results had misinterpreted the numbers.

Even during that brief, devastating period, I tried to keep my spirits up and keep my sense of humor. I told Blair, "Don't buy me a Christmas gift that will last more than six months." She didn't think it was funny.

I completed the chemo around Christmas time, and in January of 1992 I began six weeks of radiation treatments. My hoped-for return to work in April was now postponed until July.

The effects of my illness were just as hard on Blair as they were on me. The caretaker always has a heavy burden, and the patient does not always realize or understand that. While I was focused on my illness, and trying to get better, Blair had taken on more work at the practice and more of the household duties, while also dealing with her own fears and emotions revolving around my illness. When she tried to talk to me about those feelings, I tended to shut her down. This just frustrated her more and made her angry. It was very stressful for both of us.

We tried hard not to let the illness change the way we related to each other, and to be honest about our feelings. I didn't want her to "baby" me because I was sick, even though I sometimes used it as an excuse. One night in particular stands out, when she came home exhausted from a long day at work, to find dishes stacked in the sink, counters dirty, and the kitchen in general disarray. She yelled at me about not cleaning up after myself. My response was, "I've had a busy day, and besides ... I have cancer!" The writer for the Press-Enterprise who chronicled my cancer journey in the paper quickly quoted that experience. Blair reported many encouraging remarks from patients who experienced similar and many other situations we talked about. She was right to be honest in her feelings. It doesn't help to project a false image in the relationship just because one person is ill.

Though my recovery was still progressing, I wasn't able to return to work in July as I had hoped, and I missed practicing. I attended several conferences to stay abreast of new advances in medicine, but I was itching to get back to the office. I especially missed the patients. Sometimes I would see them around town, and they would give me a hug, or a word of encouragement. It felt strange to be on the receiving end of that, since I was used to being the one offering encouraging words. I was now seeing things from the patient's point of view, and it was good for me.

That September, 1992, Shally left for college. Now all the kids were off on their own, and the two of us were rambling around in a much-too-big, six-bedroom house. We also weren't sure what my prognosis was, and thought it might be better to downsize, in case it became necessary for Blair to take care of a place on her own. We decided to sell the Orangeville home and build a smaller house in Bloomsburg.

As we were having the house appraised, I casually said, "If you have anyone interested in a six-bedroom house, bring them over. The next week she did, and two weeks later it was sold. The buyers wanted to move in by mid-November, and so we needed to move quickly. Around the same time, our former babysitter called and said she was moving out of her trailer, and asked if we might want to buy it. Since our new house wouldn't be completed until spring at the earliest, we bought the trailer and moved in.

By January 1993, I was doing much better, and finally returned to work. The cancer had been in remission since the previous April, and if it remained that way for five years, I'd be considered cured. I still wasn't out of the woods, but things were moving in the right direction.

I was back, but had to drastically cut my hours down from what I had been doing two years ago, when I thought nothing of working 60 to 80 hours a week. Now I promised Blair I'd limit my work week to 20 hours. It wasn't a difficult promise to keep, since I still didn't have the stamina I'd once had. A side-effect of the chemo and radiation is that it can cause pulmonary fibrosis, a lung condition that results in a shortness of breath. I would tire easily, and needed to rest more often. It was frustrating—but I considered the alternative, and was thankful to be alive.

Blair ...
I had been sharing call on a regular basis, and I had been involved in many community activities. David had been the face of our practice. He was delivering 150 babies a year, and of course he spent many long hours at the hospital. I sought my persona in community service. I ran for the school board and, unexpectedly, won. Of course the Revak name probably assisted me in gaining votes. I even performed CPR on a visitor to a board meeting one night.

I was active in the American Association of University Women. We started the Women's center, including housing for abused women. I was involved in the creation of a federally funded day care center for children of working low-income mothers. And I could not enroll my children in the center. I was active in our church serving on the council.

As I completed my tenure as Medical Staff President I went on to serve on several committees for the Pennsylvania Medical Society. I was on the leadership committee and gave testimony to the Pennsylvania Congress on Advance Directive/Living Will Legislation. It was after one of those meetings that I fell on ice as I approached my car, fracturing my ankle. An extended stay in a hospital in Harrisburg led me home with a plate and nine screws in my ankle.

Just before we made the decision to leave Bloomsburg and move west, several docs in the society encouraged me to run for President of the Pennsylvania Medical Society. I had been the first woman President of my Medical Staff and the first woman President of the Columbia County Medical Society. Now an opportunity to become the first woman President of the Pennsylvania Medical Society was rejected, as David and I had decided to move west.

With the Medical Society's nomination, I was appointed by the governor to the Pennsylvania Board of Medicine. I spent two terms helping to advance medicine in Pennsylvania and provide leadership in disciplining physicians.

I remember vividly, while president of our hospital Medical, telling a physician to "get a life" when he asked to miss meetings to take his children to the school bus. Many years earlier I'd had to take only partial medical staff privileges, as I had three children under the age of five and could not attend the regular staff meetings as required.

I must say, it was rare that I experienced discrimination as a woman in medicine. I spent many wonderful years shoulder-to-shoulder with the men with whom I provided patient care.

David ...

Later that year we moved into our newly completed home, which backed up to the park in Bloomsburg. We loved it, but it was much smaller than what we had been used to, and it wasn't long before Blair said, "Well, if you're going to live, I want a bigger house."

The truth was, the kids were starting families of their own, and we just needed more room when they all came to visit. And so in the spring of 1996 we moved again.

This home sat on the side of a hill overlooking the town of Bloomsburg. We paid about $205,000 for it, and it would probably be valued at around a million dollars in Arizona. It consisted of three levels, with a huge bar-room in the basement.

We were in our new home, I was back at work, and life was looking bright again. We had done some traveling the previous year, taking a Caribbean cruise and a trip to Europe and England. Odd as it might sound, I can reflect back on the cancer as a blessing. It made me look around and see what was truly important in life, and to appreciate what I had. I was a better doctor for having been in the patient's shoes. And I worried less, since I'd now come through one the biggest worries people face. I wouldn't want to go through it again, but the insight I gained almost made it worthwhile.

Above: March 1992

Right: Back to work, 1993

Below: With David's parents

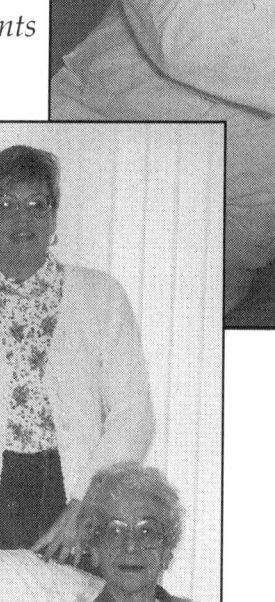

Chapter 16
Winding up the Practice

DAVID ...

I had settled back into a work routine, and remained cancer-free, which was a blessing, and a huge relief. The kids were all on their own, either married or in college. When they were in college, we'd buy a house for them to live in, then rent it out when they graduated and moved on. It was an investment for us, and a savings for them.

Our practice was still doing well, and I was also serving as the Bloomsburg jail doctor, which I did for about fifteen years. I got a kick out of listening to all the "innocent" people bemoaning their unjust fate. I loved to tease them about their innocence, but they didn't get angry at me. You can say just about anything if you say it with a smile. I would laugh and kid around with them, so they didn't take offense, but they still insisted they were not guilty.

On the other hand, some individuals intentionally committed a misdemeanor just so they could hang out in jail for thirty days. They'd stay warm, eat well, and get their medical problems attended to.

We had been renting an office downtown for a couple of years, and around 1994 we built our own office near the hospital. Drs. Bill Kuprevich and Jody Hutson were still with us, and in 1997, we brought in two more partners; Drs. Chris and Catherine O'Neill. This was especially fulfilling for me, because Blairanne and I had been friends of the O'Neil family since Chris was a child. I had mentored him, and when he was about thirteen I started encouraging him to go to medical school. He did, and even attended the same medical school I had gone to—and he also married a doctor. When the couple joined our practice, it seemed everything had come full circle.

By the mid-1990s, HMOs were becoming more pervasive, and the complex paperwork took time away from seeing patients. It was also becoming more difficult to practice without being part of the hospital system.

So in 1998, when we had an offer from Bloomsburg Hospital to buy our practice, we took it. We hadn't really wanted to sell, but we saw it as a way to eliminate some of the headaches. We were paid for it over a three year period, and we stayed on as employees of Family Care Associates, receiving a salary from the hospital. As it turned out, it was not a good deal for us. And in addition we were beginning to look toward retirement from Bloomsburg. We saw a possibility of moving west and working on different Indian Reservations. We were seeing more patients, making less money, and now we had to go through the hospital for everything we needed.

We'd had a very successful practice, but now our expenses were going up, because we had to pay the hospital for things we had been doing ourselves. After the first year, we asked for $150,000 for each of us for three years. The hospital refused, so we left. They soon realized they'd made a mistake by not granting our request, because now they had to pay four people to do what the two of us had been doing. Since I was also a DO, I had been able to do manipulations and other procedures that a general MD didn't do. The hospital administrator later told us they realized after the fact they should have convinced us to stay.

The HMO was not necessarily a good thing—at least not from the physician's standpoint. People began coming in and wanting everything imaginable to be fixed. I used to tell them, "If you lived two lifetimes you couldn't have that many problems."

Under the HMO guidelines, we could not drop a patient if he or she was abusive, but they could "fire" us. Some of my patients did just that, because they didn't like my directness. For those who came into the office upset, we just did the best we could to diffuse the situation.

There are many changes in medicine that people don't take into consideration. The average male physician used to work about 60 to 70 hours a week, while the average female only worked about 30 hours. Men will make a career out of medicine, but women don't necessarily. However, on the flip side; the men will die or retire sooner, while those women who do make a career of it, will often practice until they're in their seventies.

More and more women are becoming cardiologists, dentists, and other specialists, and they're good. They spend extra time with a patient, and take good care of them. But because they typically see fewer patients, and are working shorter hours, we'll need many more physicians to keep up with the demand.

By 2001, we were unhappy working for the hospital, and decided it was time to end our practice. Our three-year contract with the hospital was up, and it felt like the right time to leave. It was not an easy decision, because—except for the two years on the reservation—our thirty-year practice in Bloomsburg had been our life.

We looked back on those early months when we arrived fresh out of medical school and opened our first office on Market Street. We paid $150 a month rent, started out with twenty patients, and charged five dollars for an office visit.

Now we had four associates working with us, our office had 13 examining rooms, and we were serving over 16,000 patients. I had delivered over 3,500 babies in twenty years, and was now seeing the children of the children I had delivered!

Our office manager, Helen Hock, and office worker Kay Martenas had started with us at the very beginning, and were still with us. It would be hard to leave our co-workers and all the patients we had come to know over the thirty years.

But it was time for a change. We were leaving our practice, but we weren't retiring. We were thinking about doing more volunteer work with the Indians. We thought we'd travel around the country some, and sightsee. Our daughter Heather was living in Arizona, and we planned a visit to her. In June of 2001, we turned the practice over to the O'Neil's, said goodbye to family and friends … and headed west.

David Revak, D.O.
Family Practice

Your friend for life in Bloomsburg

Dr. David Revak was one semester short of a degree in Accounting when work at an area home for retarded citizens convinced him he would be better working with people, not numbers.

"In the back of my mind, I guess I was always thinking about Medicine as a career. I was really impressed with the family physicians we had in Mt. Carmel. My experiences in working at that home just helped me redirect my energies," said the father of five.

After graduation from Susquehanna University and Philadelphia College of Osteopathic Medicine, he and his wife, Blairanne Revak, M.D., set up a joint practice in Bloomsburg.

"Dr. Ritmiller recruited both of us to come to The Bloomsburg Hospital. We opened the office in July 1971. We are still seeing some of the same patients we saw during our first week," the former college football player said.

"When we joined the medical staff, the hospital was working on getting an Intensive Care Unit. Now, its size was recently doubled. Change is inevitable. The area is not as rural as it used to be, it's suburban. But, thankfully, both the town of Bloomsburg and The Bloomsburg Hospital haven't lost that small town touch."

Dr. Revak, who is in practice with his wife and Dr. William Kuprevich, said the three of them, each with their own unique personality attracting different types of patients, work well together.

"I am really very serious. I mask my sensitivity with very gregarious behavior. Some people say I laugh too much. But, what's the alternative? To me, humor is one of life's great recuperative forces."

THE BLOOMSBURG HOSPITAL

Left & Right: "Your friend for life in Bloomsburg" articles published for both David and Blair in the Bloomsburg newspaper.

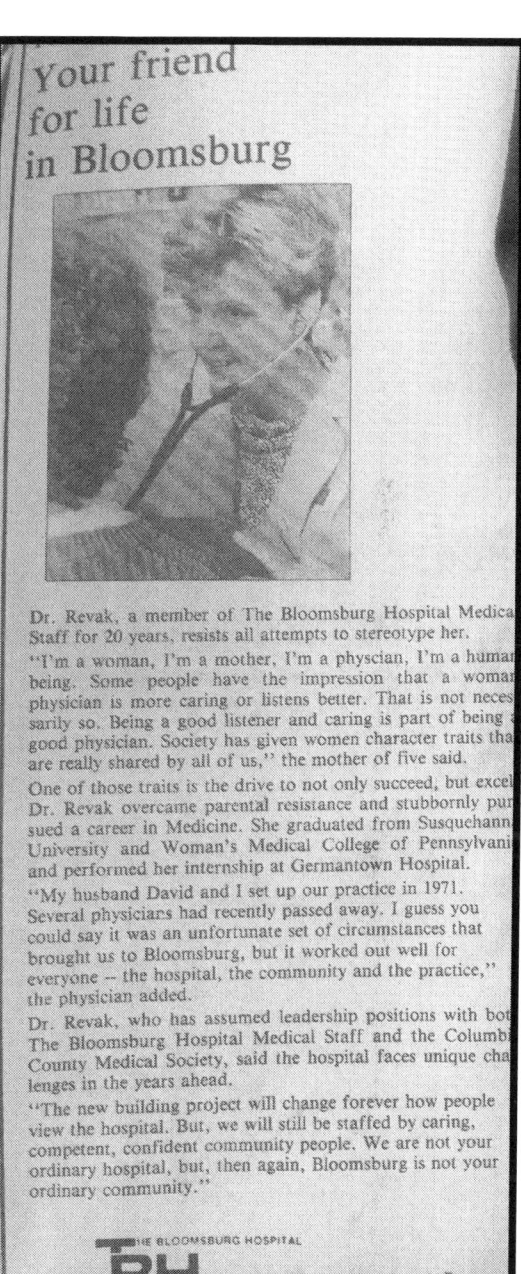

Your friend for life in Bloomsburg

Dr. Revak, a member of The Bloomsburg Hospital Medical Staff for 20 years, resists all attempts to stereotype her.

"I'm a woman, I'm a mother, I'm a physcian, I'm a human being. Some people have the impression that a woman physician is more caring or listens better. That is not necessarily so. Being a good listener and caring is part of being a good physician. Society has given women character traits that are really shared by all of us," the mother of five said.

One of those traits is the drive to not only succeed, but excel. Dr. Revak overcame parental resistance and stubbornly pursued a career in Medicine. She graduated from Susquehanna University and Woman's Medical College of Pennsylvania and performed her internship at Germantown Hospital.

"My husband David and I set up our practice in 1971. Several physicians had recently passed away. I guess you could say it was an unfortunate set of circumstances that brought us to Bloomsburg, but it worked out well for everyone — the hospital, the community and the practice," the physician added.

Dr. Revak, who has assumed leadership positions with both The Bloomsburg Hospital Medical Staff and the Columbia County Medical Society, said the hospital faces unique challenges in the years ahead.

"The new building project will change forever how people view the hospital. But, we will still be staffed by caring, competent, confident community people. We are not your ordinary hospital, but, then again, Bloomsburg is not your ordinary community."

THE BLOOMSBURG HOSPITAL
BH Your friends for life.

Hospital recertified

Dr. Blairann Revak, left, president of Bloomsburg Hospital's medical staff, and Robert Spinelli, hospital administrator, stand in front of a certificate received recently from the Joint Commission on Accreditation of Healthcare Organization. The three-year accreditation is the result of a voluntary inspection of the hospital's performance in complying with national standards designed to result in high employee performances and reduced patient risk. The certificate is on display in the hospital's main lobby.

Kudos for Blair

DAVID REVAK

⇐ *Clowning Around* ⇑

Chapter 17
Retirement

DAVID ...

We were now retired from our practice, but had no plans to stop working. We had talked about volunteering on a reservation again, but didn't want to make another two-year commitment. Since we had no permanent place to be, and we wanted to travel as much as possible, we decided to buy an RV that we could drive around and live in as well. We had owned a couple of others through the years, and enjoyed the freedom they allow.

Years before, we had purchased a lot by a creek, and rather than build on it, we bought a 23-foot motorhome and left it on that lot during most of the year. Other times we'd drive to Florida in it, and park it on the sea shore. With five kids, we still had bodies sleeping on the floor, but we always had a great time.

We had only paid $7,000 for that one, and then paid $13,000 for our second one. This last one—our retirement RV—was 34 feet long; big enough for us to live in for a while, and we paid $93,000 for it. I'd had a Jaguar that I had bought at a discounted price because it was a repo, and I traded that in and got $40,000 allowance for it. So the motorhome only cost us about another $50,000, and we paid that off in less than three years.

We had seen our last patients in June, then prepared the RV for our trip. We spent about a month driving to Arizona, visiting family and friends along the way, and relaxing in the Phoenix area. Then we took off on our first assignment.

We were working with Project USA as volunteer physicians. We got travel expenses plus a stipend of about $800 - $1,000 a week. They would call and ask if we could go spend a few weeks somewhere as a vacation replacement, and off we'd go. Other times we'd stay in one place for several months before moving on to the next one. It was a great lifestyle, and we were having a good time, while still feeling like we were contributing something worthwhile. We lived and traveled in that RV for a couple of years, driving through North Dakota, South Dakota, New Mexico and Arizona, working on different reservations as we went.

Our first assignment took us to Eagle Butte, South Dakota, where we worked in a clinic for the Cheyenne River Sioux. This was in the north central part of the state, and the wind blew constantly. The day we arrived there it was 102 degrees, and the wind was blowing at 35 mph. This reservation was very isolated, with the nearest shopping mall being 150 miles away in Rapid City.

Eagle Butte is pretty much an all-Indian town, and unfortunately, we saw lots of corruption there. It seemed as though the residents wanted a total welfare system. No one owned anything, nor took pride in anything.

We worked normal Monday through Friday hours, and then would leave every Friday night for the weekend. We'd often go to Pierre, a small town with a population of about 12,000. You could camp along the river for a donation, and we did that when the weather was nice. On Sundays we'd visit a Lutheran church, and we did as much sightseeing as we could; visiting Mount Rushmore, the Crazy Horse Monument, and the Black Hills area.

We were in Eagle Butte on September 11, 2001, when terrorists attacked our country, and we all shared the same reactions of shock, anxiety and loss. Many of the Sioux people have served in the military, and felt the same devastation that Blair and I were feeling.

By the second week of November, Eagle Butte was getting pretty cold, so we headed back to Arizona where Heather was living. We decided we liked Arizona in the winter, so looked around for a house in Gilbert. When we found the one at 1837 E. Monarch Bay Drive, we stopped looking. The back yard butted up against a waterway, and it was a beautiful setting. We went back to Pennsylvania for our furniture and hauled it to Gilbert.

After getting the house settled, we returned to South Dakota and worked several more weeks there. Then I was asked to spend a month working at a clinic in North Dakota. This was also in a very remote, isolated area about fifty miles south of Bismarck. I flew in, but an optometrist friend who would also be working there, drove over. We'd take his car and get out during the weekends, visiting local churches, and whatever other interesting spots we could find.

I returned from North Dakota, and Blair and I took a short assignment at the Grand Canyon, where we worked for two weeks with the Havasupai and Hualapai Indians at Peach Springs. Shortly after that stint, we were called back for another four weeks. It looked like this might become an ongoing situation for this area, so I approached Indian Health Services, and told them, "You need to hire us or we're leaving."

By now, we were well into our second year of volunteering, and were working quite a lot. I felt that if they were going to keep calling us to that one particular spot, we might as well work there full-time, and get some benefits out of it. They did hire us, and I realized I should have done that early on, and we would have gotten benefits after five years. We spent a total of about seven years working with them, but only three and a half years counted toward benefits. At least we had insurance once we were hired, instead of depending on COBRA as we had been.

For a while we lived in a trailer park in Kingman, while working with the Hualapai in Peach Springs, and the Havasupai in the Grand Canyon. Since we would be working full-time for the Indian Health Services clinic, we decided to buy a house in Kingman, but we kept the house in Gilbert.

At the clinic, we worked regular 8-to-5 hours, with two other doctors. In 2005, we retired from the clinic, sold the Kingman house, and moved back to Gilbert.

Chapter 18
If I Were to Live My Life Over

*"When man loves, his answers are found
in the twilight of yesterday."*

David Revak

DAVID ...

If I were to live my life over, I wouldn't do anything differently, but I'd like to do it without the cancer. I miss running, and had hoped I could keep running into my sixties and seventies. I used to walk to work and then run home every day. I loved running through the town. But the cancer put an end to that.

One thing the cancer did for me, though, was help me get my priorities in order. When I went back to work, I rarely attended hospital meetings. The administrator would ask why not. I said "I have my family, my practice, and a list of other things to do. If I get to eat in a day I'm lucky. If going to a meeting is on that list, I'm not going.

He said that was the wrong attitude, and I said "Well, that's my attitude." Because of that, I was the only doctor who was never Chief of Staff. But I felt I had my priorities right.

So many things I used to worry about, or put too much emphasis on, I've discovered, just aren't important. Right now I'm at that stage where I don't want to do anything I don't want to do. I have my own priorities. I'll take the time to set up a liquor cabinet, but I don't need to go to a meeting at church.

I may have a year, five years, maybe fifteen, I don't know. I take nine pills in the morning, three in the evening, and I'm on oxygen. But I want to enjoy the last few years I have. I want to travel … maybe go to Florida for a couple of months in the winter. And when I'm home, I'm happy to just be here. I mow, do yard work, and do all the cooking. I listen to Rush Limbaugh, and all the conservative radio. I'm happy. Blairanne has things she enjoys; her clinic, Toastmasters … and I'm happy doing what I do.

I've had to overcome some challenges in my life; the cancer being one of the biggest. But even before that, I had to overcome all the negativity I grew up with. My parents fought all the time, and it was hard living with that. They fought over religion, and they fought over money. Having bill collectors constantly hounding us was depressing and could wear me down, but somehow I always knew I was going to be successful. I knew that the "American Dream" was … if you work hard, you will succeed. And I was always a hard worker.

Probably the one thing that got me through all the tough times was my ability to laugh about everything. I could laugh at myself, and I could make others laugh. Even after the diagnosis of cancer, I could make jokes about it. One of our family photos shows me making faces, acting out. I will almost always screw up any photo I'm in, just being silly.

In addition to laughter, two words have meant a lot to me over the years: Vicissitudes and Serendipity.

Vicissitudes refers to those changes in life that you have no control over. You're walking down the street, a car jumps the curb and cripples or kills you. It's not your fault, and there's nothing you can do about it. I experienced this when I had the ear infection as a child, hurt my shoulder, and blew out my knee in high school, keeping me from playing football. My life might have taken a different turn but for these events.

Serendipity—in my case—is being in the right place at the right time. One example is my working at the Hotel Governor Snyder when Jim App mentioned that his father-in-law was a DO, and suggested I talk with him. That chance conversation set me on the path that determined my career.

I think I was a pretty good physician, and I loved going to work. If I have to say what I'm proud of, that would be one thing. I wanted to practice until I was in my nineties, but that didn't work out. I always felt it was important to give back, and Blairanne and I donated a lot of time to treating others for free.

Blairanne and some others started a women's clinic in Pennsylvania, and once a month, I would treat their patients. We would do IUDs and pap smears, put them on birth control ... and we did it all for free. Then the Geisinger Medical

Center came in, put residents in charge of it, paid them salaries and started charging everybody. It was a welfare clinic, then it became part of medicaid and we were out.

I volunteered with the school sports programs, doing physicals for the football teams and the little league. Two of us would see fifty kids in a day. We'd examine them, listen to their hearts, refer them to the cardiologist if they had a murmur, refer them to their family doctor if necessary, and it was all free.

We never turned anyone away because they couldn't pay. Probably thirty percent of the people we saw in our office never paid. I was making a good living. You've got to give back.

I think I would have been a good Chief of Staff, too, because I was good at getting to the heart of the matter. When the doctors or staff would get into a hassle at a meeting, I'd stand up and say, "What's important here? You're talking, you're talking, everybody's asking 'What should we do?' Just make a decision!"

The administrator would say, sarcastically, "Why don't you tell us what you think, Dr. Revak."

I was also good at handling conflict. If two people were at odds, I'd get them both together and get their stories while they were face-to-face. I learned that the stories changed from what they'd been telling others. My dad always said "There's this story and there's that story, and somewhere in the middle is the truth." I could usually get at the truth and get the problem resolved.

I'm also proud of my kids, and glad that none of them are in jail. I'd like them to go to church, I'd like them to be more open, and I'd like them to be more academic.

If I were to advise them, I'd say you've got to plan your life, and you've got to have alternatives. What influenced my life plan was the bill collectors. I knew I had to have money, and I had to have things. Even in high school I knew that money was power; a means to success, a position in life, and people.

If you say you're a physician, right away you get respect. I don't care who I meet—a Senator, a doctor, whatever—I treat them as I would treat you, or as I would treat someone who is mentally challenged, because I learned they can relate as well as a Senator.

I'd also tell my kids, you've got to stand for what you believe in, be fair and be honest. You've got to have values and stand by them. I don't care if they're liberal values or conservative values, but you'd better believe in them, and you'd better not be working it.

As far as my political beliefs, I think the conservative way is the best way to go. I think the Republicans should drop this crap about abortion and gays. Gays are good people. Let them have their civil unions. I don't know if they could be married in a church, if the church doesn't approve of it, but that's not important. Let them get married. Give them the benefits. If a woman wants to have an abortion, let her have it.

I probably think of myself more as a Libertarian. I believe we should be allowed to own and carry a gun, and I do. I'm not gonna be the guy who goes and shoots other people, but I can protect myself and others if I need to. And I think if you want to use drugs, use them. But if you kill somebody while using them, then you deserve to be killed. If you're drunk and kill a child, you need to pay for that. I have nothing against vigilantism, as long as it's done legally.

I also have strong feelings about the black issue. I think black leaders keep black people down. They suppress them, repress them, and tell them "whitey will not allow you to achieve." We have an expanding black middle class.

You can't have handouts, and welfare is a handout. Churches will provide for people. Forty-seven percent of the people are getting some kind of government subsidy. Seventy-two cents of every welfare dollar goes for the administration of the program, to provide pensions and salaries for union workers making a hundred thousand dollars a year. We're a free enterprise country, we've got to let the market level.

The clinic Blairanne has been working with is now part of the federal government. They've done away with the get-togethers, the volunteer things where you can go have lunch and meet people. They took the personality out of the Methodist clinic. Now they're a welfare clinic. Blairanne can't see anybody for free, she can only see the walk-ins that aren't free.

The U.S. government has got to stop. They're taking all the goodness out of people to the point where you expect somebody to care for your ass. Americans are the greatest givers in the world, but we're going to destroy that in the generation we're raising now, because they're going to expect to be taken care of.

I don't belong to any organizations. I didn't like the Moose or the Elks. I felt that they were anti-black. When I went to Bloomsburg, I was asked if I was a Mason. I said I wasn't, and they said, "Well you need to join the Masons or you'll never make it here." I wouldn't join, and I made it just fine.

I belong to a Lutheran church because I think the basic philosophy is there; that through the grace of God is the only way to get saved. It has nothing to do with good works, and all that Mormon philosophy.

A scripture says: Again I say to you, it is easier for a camel to pass through the eye of a needle than for one who is rich to enter the kingdom of God. Matthew 19:23

It's almost as if we're not supposed to be wealthy, and yet it's the American dream to acquire. That's what's great about America. All these millionaires and billionaires; Carnegie, Rockefeller, Bill Gates, Warren Buffet … what do they do with their money? They give it away! Just one percent of the people make the really big bucks. About one out of six people in America have a net worth of $1 million. The rest make $150,000 to $200,000 tops. We can't help others if we don't have the money to do it with.

It's not that hard to become a millionaire. Farmers, nurses, teachers, people with average-paying jobs become millionaires, because they know how to save and how to spend wisely. If a two-wage-earning couple can live on one salary and put the other away, they could put away thirty-thousand or more a year for several years, and by retirement they could be millionaires.

I believe anyone can become wealthy if they're willing to work for it, and if they're smart with their money and their time. I always had at least one job—sometimes two or three—while in high school and college. In college I'd buy or find junk furniture, fix it up and sell it for extra money. Even my hobbies have always been investments: Antiques, paintings, coins, and stamps. I've always lived frugally, and I always had money. I graduated from both college and medical school with thousands in cash. When Blairanne and I graduated from med school we were able to buy a new Volkswagen. We had bonds we cashed in, and we always had emergency cash.

Being retired and living in Arizona has brought a sense of anonymity to my life, that I enjoy. When I came out here by myself the first time, no one knew me, and I was happy.

I love to read, and like to paint, but I do it for myself, no one else. I enjoy writing, and wrote poetry and essays in college. I wrote poems to Blair while we were dating. I'm interested in politics, or anything interesting. I've always had a curious mind. And I'd love to travel more. Blair and I traveled when we could, venturing to Israel and Eastern

Europe in 1998, and going on an Alaskan cruise in 2005. I love seeing new places and experiencing other cultures.

I've had a full life, and would do it all over again, but would want to know what I was doing the second time around. I always had good mentors and good friends.

Blairanne and I have been lovers, partners in our practice, and best friends. We're like two peas in a pod, and still love being together. When I was a kid, I swore I'd never fight over religion, money, or anything, and we never have. To this day, we don't fight.

Chapter 19
Cancer Comes Again

"Six Months to Live: Will I See Christmas? Which Christmas?"

BLAIR...
For our story, I write the last two years of David's life.

We got almost two years from David's diagnosis in February 2012 to his death on January 30, 2014. Let's look at that last almost-two years. I do remember huge amounts of time driving to and parking at the MD Anderson clinic. Huge numbers of hours sitting and waiting. Huge numbers of hours with the comfort of togetherness. And yes, huge numbers of hours when I said this is awful, this is so bad for him. And he never complained once. And I never was sensitive enough to read all the pain, nausea, and anxiety he suffered.

I am constantly reminded of the Cardinals vs. LA Rams football game we attended in December of 2013, maybe 6 weeks before he died and 3 weeks before we went to Hospice care. We had a wheelchair and he could get out to walk the dog with me pushing, and we could attend Cardinals games. He loved those games. The game was tied and there were five minutes on the clock. He pulled my eyes to him as the crowd stood watching and waiting in the roar of "can we win this one?" He directed me, "Take me to the car."

I was shocked, I was in disbelief and argued, "It is a tie score, we will miss the last five minutes, the most important ..."

"Take me to the car," he repeated.

"Oh, okay, is something wrong?" I questioned.

His response was only, "Take me to the car."

No discussion, no explanation ever followed. At the car we sat quietly catching the last minute of the game—and the loss—on the radio. How ill he was, I do not know.

It was in Guatemala that he complained of stomach distress and spent the day in bed, saying, "I'm okay, you go with the tour. We had one more day in Guatemala and then the flight back to Miami. It was the cross-country Interstate 10 drive to Gilbert that worried me. I looked up flights, I agonized over the 3-hour trip to the airport. Will he be okay? Is it his gall bladder? We knew he had stones in the gall bladder. They were always reported when he had a scan for the lungs and the follow up of the Hodgkins Disease, and then the pulmonary fibrosis problem with his lungs.

We made it to Miami, and en route home we visited the Camplese, cousin Sue, and then made our first stop near Pensacola Florida. We walked the beach, which that afternoon was covered with blue, blown-up man-of-wars; a huge invasion. We found a beachside seafood house and enjoyed the clams, oysters and beer.

David ate his oysters raw, letting them literally slide down his throat. Later, when the difficulty with swallowing became more evident...he reminded me he was able to eat oysters that week. "Yes," I said, "you let them slide down your throat."

I know he had been eating little for months. He insisted he had to lose weight. A favorite food was grapes. They, too, slide down the throat, don't they? So how long the tumor had been growing in his esophagus is an unanswerable question, but one thing is for sure, it was growing during that year.

The trip home was pretty short; two overnights on the I -10 and we were home. On one occasion he complained of shortness of breath, his oxygen levels were pretty low, with no explanation, but it passed during the day.

We were home one week when he complained again about his abdomen and I called for an appointment with Dr. Griner. That was a five-day delayed appointment. The next week he was so weak, and so sick-looking I called for an earlier appointment with Dr. Udall. I went in to the bed when he wakened and asked how he was. He replied his abdomen was bothering him. I examined it and found an acute abdomen. "What would you tell a patient to do if they had this abdomen," I asked.

He replied, "Go to the ER."

We did. The urgent ultrasound showed nodules in the liver. He was partially obstructed and it was decided to remove the gall bladder. The biopsy of the nodules showed undifferentiated cells with no origin evident. So the plan was a GI workup. Getting an appointment was one delay after another, though the surgeon said he would be called by MD Anderson. We found an appointment with Dr. DeRoot at Ironwood Cancer Center. The surgeon called and got David scheduled for an EGD, which confirmed the esophageal origin of the cancer. A PET scan suggested the nodules in the liver, four or five of them, and an area in the scapula, or in the soft tissue over the scapula, were the sites of the cancer. Dr. De Root immediately began chemo.

I journaled from the time we were in Florida until now, and wrote a good bit of information during that time. I have no memory of any of it. I may go back and read some of it to try and insert some in this writing. Simply put, it was on again-off again chemo almost the entire time he lived. There were times he was so diarrhead out that he couldn't walk and ended up in the hospital for six days, and there were times he looked healthy. He always went to the MD Anderson clinic dressed well and neat, and he always talked like he was doing fine (many times I inserted other observations during his visits.)

He always knew and attended more to his caregivers than most people would, and always entertained everybody. He painted, starting in the second month of his chemo, I think, and expanded that vocation to many hours of daily "meditation and prayer," as he said.

Painting became a vital part of the cancer treatment course. Daily, he would rise and take his time dressing and sitting on the bed petting Zaydie. She never left the room if he was in it. After he was dressed he would say, "Want some lovin?" and she would jump on the bed as he petted her. He rose and dressed every day that he could. He would then take Zaydie for a walk.

We reached the point, probably winter to spring of 2013, when Eric convinced him to get a wheelchair. He refused my suggestion, but Eric has a wonderful, shared, caring-for-disabled-people understanding that fell into his discussion with David.

When David had been walking, he had stopped and sat on the tree branches near the ground about 100 yards from home, and then sat at the base of the power line to make the journey. Now I could push and he could just smell the roses. So often we would get to the greenway and he would say, "let's go smell the roses." He enjoyed that so much. The wheelchair became his transit to the Cardinal stadium and it was used for many games he attended, with disabled seating. Great way for Heather

Adam and I to get into the game and quickly out with his wheelchair. Priority elevator rides were in the bunch.

The painting began suddenly, about two months after he began chemo. I think it was before his hospitalization from severe diarrhea, but he started up quickly after he was able to do it. He did not talk about it, he just started.

I was always on him to be busy, to be doing something. And that was a product of my acknowledgement that he had such talent. And to not be busy is a waste of time to me. He was encumbered by the pulmonary fibrosis. He was on continuous oxygen and did well with it. I think he often had to rest in spite of the oxygen, but he never complained or related that he "couldn't do". When he started chemo he had been doing 3000 abdominal crunches almost daily. His fitness was so important.

With the painting, he isolated himself and told us he did it as meditation and as prayer with God. Meditation was listening to God, Prayer was talking to God. When he was painting, the world around did not seem to exist. It was his private time from me also. The only time I got painting discussion from him was if I sat down with the painting and questioned him. And then he often did not have answers. That is why when he did that last painting, Madonna with No Arms, and three times said, "she has no arms," I was so startled.

"Why didn't you put on the arms? You can still give her arms? What does it mean?"

He was so sick at the time he could barely print his name. He never gave me an answer about the "meaning" of the Madonna painting. But the fact that he named it to me three times told me he was saying something special. But what was he saying? To this day I ruminate and wonder. Maybe I am to be those arms. Maybe he could no longer hold and support me. Maybe he was saying something I should read in that painting. I wish I knew.

There were recurring themes in his paintings. He painted his interpretations of friends, including Don Camplese, Joe Hilgar, Bill and Jane Gittler, Kay Camplese, and Lou and Diane O'Neil, all our best friends. Those paintings he sent to them personally. I have all the rest of the paintings except the one he gave to Dr. Dragovich.

As soon as he began painting, most of the first works were cancer-related issues. Themes that rang through were the three crosses and the three crows, Emmet Kelley, the clown, the red line that represented the red line of MDAnderson bill board ads, and eyes watching or looking at us. He also used the two men with hats who always looked to me like they were falling. He characterized these two men as the other people looking at the cancer patient saying, "glad it is not me."

He felt strongly about that unique isolation created by the cancer diagnosis. He even titled several paintings around the term Isolation.

David was always on stage in his life. So this may have been a negative view of that experience. His characterization of self was each day as he rose to go to work saying, "It's Showtime," and he behaved all his life as if he were on stage.

He started with oils I had bought him three years earlier, pushing him to try painting with a package of canvases. Then I found a lot of acrylics at the thrift store and bought those. He liked using spray cans and even decorated frames with the spray paints. Often he used them as his base coat before painting, we also bought a lot of prints and frames at thrift stores, as they provided a low-cost finish to the paintings. The Madonna with No Arms is the only painting he did not frame and I think that was because it was an awkward shape and he was so sick at the time.

During the on-again-off-again chemotherapy, he would have times of strength to go to events and visit. He always went to church, except the day he said, "Let's stay home," as he said he was a little weak. He then proceeded to try to get out of his chair and flew forward across the coffee table, sliding unresponsively between his recliner and the sofa. He appeared to arrest with no responsiveness for a good 30 seconds, and then began to respond. I could find no pulse. I called 911, Shally, and Heather, and they responded within five minutes. His blood pressure was 40-50 systolic and stayed in that range even after 3000 cc of fluids. After about 36 hours he began a blood pressure response and clear consciousness. The hospitalist announced it was time to discontinue chemo. I never heard a diagnosis.

David talked to all four of the grandchildren here, and said later he thought he was "a goner." Other than the early chemo dehydration diarrhea, he did not require another hospitalization. And he tolerated all the treatments pretty well. Wrong; he did have two days in the hospital when he developed a bacteremia. He was cold and his temp was 99.8 and later 100.2. I called and asked if we could go to the lab for a draw about 3 p.m. The nurse wanted him to go to the ER, but he said no, so they consented to outpatient labs. Next morning at 7:30 they called for him to go to the ER as cultures were already positive. The test for sepsis was negative, so he did well getting started on the IV Rocephin, which we continued at home for 30 days after his discharge. I was able to give the every-twelve-hour intravenous antibiotic, fortunately, so he was able to stay home. He continued to paint then also. He knew all the nurses by name, and they all liked him. He was told they fought over who would get to care for him.

During all this time, he ate minimal food. In fact, Zaydie probably was his food outlet, as she ate most of the food we/I thought David was eating. He always refused nutritional liquids, as I tried everything I could find that came with any nutritional boosting on the label. He simply hated the taste of all of them. I thought I would have drunk them just to keep me going. He had none of that.

For that period of time, our house ran on a routine. He was usually able to get out and do most things we wanted to do, including Shakespeare plays, football games, basketball (ASU) and horse races with Blix and his friend Bill, who owned and raced horses.

Life was pretty serious, but he did pull fast ones and make fun. My favorite story to tell is how he refused my solution for his diarrhea when I purchased grey Depends for him to wear. I was trying so hard to be a good caregiver for him. When the diarrhea was so severe it was disabling him. It did result in his dehydration and a six-day hospitalization to manage it. But when he was struggling I purchased "masculine" looking gray Depends underwear. He refused. "I'm not wearing Depends", he asserted.

While sitting in the family room with Denise and Charles, 7-year old Amaya, Shally and Eric, he raced from the room. I thought, Oh, no, another episode. Shall I check on him? Moments later into the room appeared David wearing only Depends and prancing as if walking down the runway at a fashion show. Kids and all found wonderful laughter for him. And I insisted he pose for a photo. This photo became very important for me in my grief. I was in the fourth month of grieving for his loss, feeling like there was no laughter available in my life when I picked up that photo of David modeling Depends and laughed. Yes, I could still laugh, and yes I would make it through this loss.

He sent his usual 50 cards per week, and always had a pack ready to mail. Copies and copies of photos were used to send post cards to everyone we knew. He had done this for years, starting back in 1981 when we were on the reservation. The cards were noted to be unreadable by anyone. In fact, cousin Tony told us he took one to his pharmacist and asked him if he could read it, since David was a doctor. If you visited us, or if we visited you, David always had a camera as part of his wardrobe, and he snapped photos. In fact, while traveling with Fran and Dee he would frequently call to Dee and me, "turn around girls," so he could take a photo. And we then became known as the "turn around girls."

As a result of his face behind the camera, there are limited photos with him as the subject. We have thousands of photos, and I have boxes and boxes of photos he created, as he made doubles and triples to mail out. He left me at least five photo boxes of extras to dispense with. He never had or wanted a phone to take photos with; his camera was part of his gear.

When they stopped the chemo after his episode of hypotension and hospitalization, I questioned Dr. Dragovich about going to hospice care. He delayed, and then came into the room saying he wanted to have the radiation people consider treating the liver lesions with injections of yttrium directly into the liver. As I researched it, I learned it is the new technique for treating liver cancer, especially that resulting from Hepatitis C. By mapping the arterial supply to the liver with dyes they can inject pebules of radiation directly into the blood vessel feeding a tumor, and decrease or obliterate the lesion. The radiation doc said he was a candidate, as the CT scan demonstrated the cancer activity only in the liver. We waited Medicare/BC BS approval, as I asked what was the cost if they denied coverage. "Is it over $25,000," I asked.

His response, "More like $200.000.00."

We talked about the specialty of the care, the cost, the sense of guilt we both shared about being possibly selected for this procedure. The cost could probably build a hospital and staff it in many parts of the world. Then we saw the movie, Captain Phillips. The cost of the armies of several countries, the munitions, the specialty work done to rescue one man taken hostage by pirates, was clearly phenomenal. Someone told me our culture is unique to focus on and spend phenomenal money and resources for one human. We felt a little better about our notice that Medicare consented to cover the radiation treatment for David.

The treatment began in November with a procedure in the x-ray department to map the arterial supply to the liver. Two weeks later they injected the yttrium into the liver. The doc was pleased with the procedure, saying David's vessels were a little different and they actually treated three-fourths of the liver rather than the one-half usually accomplished the first time.

The plan was to go back and do the second injection in four weeks, which fell over Christmas. They had to delay it, as it was not possible to ship the radioactive drug across the country (apparently produced in Massachusetts) over the holidays, so he was scheduled for Jan 7. In the meantime, he started to weaken. I saw progressive deterioration in his health, his strength and his functioning. They said he would be tired. I insisted it was worse than that.

Then on New Years Eve he was in the bathroom coughing and choking, and in the sink was grey tissue-like stuff and blood. Off to the ER we went and then to EGD, which demonstrated active lesions in the lower esophagus. That changed everything. We were now consulting hospice.

I am not certain of the date, but it was January something. The intake nurse came with another person who did not introduce herself until I pressured. She was Susan Levine the executive director of the agency. She was very interested in, and enjoyed having David tell her about, his paintings. When we said I had to pick up a prescription for which there was a significant copay, she called to get it covered under hospice. She was very easy to visit with. We all sat around the dining room table.

David joked with us and he looked okay, not debilitated. The next day the RN, whose name I cannot remember, visited and immediately set up a working rapport with David. She had a Polish name and was originally from New Jersey, so they hit it off right away.

When I told her he was sipping his codeine syrup, she instructed him as to what he needed and got him to comply with the calculated doses. She was a wonderful support and care manager for us. She answered many questions I had, including "when will he die," so we had time for Celestia to come in two weeks, rather than try to get a flight out this week.

He lasted about three weeks on hospice. The worst period was the last five days. He then was somnolent, sleeping most of the time and appearing comfortable. The kids all got to visit. Matthew had visited and gone home, then called to say he was coming and staying as long as Dad lived. He arrived three days before David died, and was so attentive to him.

Sunday afternoon David wanted to stay in bed, but he could not get comfortable. He said little, but had a brief conversation with Heather. I don't know the content of that conversation. Adam and Eric tried repeatedly to get him comfortable in the bed by piling pillows behind him, but his agitation was speaking more than I could handle.

I called the hospice number and requested a hospital bed for him. We rearranged the living room and Monday they delivered a hospital bed. I think I was more helpful with the morphine at this time and he became more comfortable.

Incidentally, I had been very slow to up the dose of his morphine, going from .50 to .75 ml rather than 1.0 ml, when Donna, the nurse, told me to increase the dose for his comfort. Such ambivalence. I wanted him here with me and alert. It was so hard to let go, and yet I don't remember being totally in contact with all of that reality. I was all wrapped in bubble wrap as I have written. Trying so hard to be loving and helpful, while watching the sting of death pulling him away, was a huge engagement. By now he was resting comfortably, not really interacting, but comfortable.

Peg and Mike had visited and were leaving for home before Sunday, but the girls asked her, if I asked her to stay, would she. She said certainly. Mike went home to take care of some business for three days and Peg helped me learn bed bathing and nursing comfort care. She sat with David at times, as did all of us.

On Wednesday evening there were episodes of irregular breathing. Alea and Heather stayed late. At one point Heather said she saw robed people outside the window, as if waiting. And in the same breath, Alea said, "Did you see them? I saw them too!"

I was curled up on the sofa, Matthew went to the bedroom and Peg was in bed. Suddenly his breathing became erratic, with long gaps of no breath. He took a deep, loud, sighing breath and as Matthew ran into the room, having heard that sound, David ceased breathing. I said "I think he has died."

Matthew later shared that when that audible breath occurred he was dreaming of shooting a gun, trying to keep people from breaking into the house.

I was stunned, just standing there in a trance-like state, unable to do anything for several moments. Then I made calls to Heather and Shally, and finally Celestia and Charles, as he was headed here the next day. I cannot write more description. My David had died. It was 1:29 a.m., January 30, 2014. It was Christian's birthday. And Christian was Poppy's boy.

This is a spontaneous insert today, December 30, 2015, while I was writing and inserting the stories about the kids. As I was writing, the kids were responding to the picture I sent to all of them of the entire family. This is the sequence of comments as they occurred. All are classical comments of David.

Denise: What a beautiful family we are!!!
Sabrina: Yes, indeed!!!
Chas: yeah, I can't wait until tomorrow
Shally: Hmmmm. I wonder why!!!!
Eric: Set
Celestia: Ok what's tomorrow???
Chas: I get better looking everyday
Eric: Spike
Celestia: Of course!

Chas: Should'a been a priest

Shally: Okay Dad Wanna see my new shoes.

Chas: Hey Junior.

Eric: How dare you fart before my wife?

Sabrina: I love all of u! I had a very bad day but love all these messages and memories. Made me smile.

Shally: I didn't know it was her turn!

Chas: Oohh, aughh, I had a bad day too..hurry pull my finger

Denise: Who wants to play cockerball??

Shally: woahh!!! Amaya does pull my finger ha ha

Celestia: LOL she was taught well!!!

Everyone ??

A Family Hallowe'en

Chapter 20
Closing Thoughts: April 26, 2016

BLAIR ...

David avoided writing a last chapter to his book. When Dee suggested he write a closing chapter he said "I can't, then I may have to die." And he didn't. She kindly created a draft of the book for his 72nd birthday, just a few months after he began chemotherapy. And he still refused to finish the task. Dee told me, "you do it."

To commit it all to paper made this a new, challenging task. Reading and visualizing many of David's comments created a painful strike of the rip tide, as I call it, of grief. And, oh, the words and hours of writing I could do as I review the life we had together. This volume could serve as an outline for the multitude of so many shared stories. You haven't heard of the collections of things we have on the walls and floor of this house, the trips of walking across England and cruising with friends and families and the wonderful times spent doing mission work in Guatemala. Please know our life was given to helping others and growing in our own shared love and the love of our wonderful kids as we traveled that path.

Now I go on. They say when you can make the transition from the "Why" of this loss to the "How" of "where will I now go," you have made progress in your life. I am continuing to search and motor through all of the possibilities of life as it stands before me. I am healthy and my "predicted" life expectancy is 84.

Already I have made a collection of David's paintings and shown them to several groups of cancer patients. I created a book of his paintings, hoping to share them with others. I have finally put a bit of myself into David's life story. And I am volunteering with Hospice of the Valley in three roles. I am on the Speakers' Bureau, I help with bereavement phone calls, and I assist with a Support Group.

Now I am living on. I am managing to do that and hoping to do more.

And, yes, I continue to have grief-filled moments as I yearn for the presence of my David.

David-isms

I'm bushed
           What's that?
                      Hit the books!

Got to have a cutch
        Did you get your ears lowered?
                What's wrong with this shirt?

I only had a small salad for lunch

              Why won't this guy move?

Good choices

        I'm going to lose 20 pounds by Christmas
                    Hey Junior!!!

We're moving west in three more years
        A good horse and saddle is all you need
I ever tell you about the guy with brown balls?

You can *marry* **it,**
    you can inherit **it,**
        or you can WORK your ass off

Creed of Unbeing

Ahh! There he be
                Who? Fool, There be nothing!
Alas, — You do not — So be.
                So Be What!
                To See
                    yet unsee
    To Feel
                    yet unfeel
    To Sense
                    yet unsense
   That be my sing.
Your sing has ring, but does
                no thing.
    Aye!   There you go.
      To Sigh
                   yet unsigh
     To Love
                   yet unlove
     To Die
                   yet undie
Stop!! You be apprehend!
Not Comprehend!
  So be
     I am begotten
            yet unborn.
                David Revak

Creed of Being

Ahh!   There he be
    Who?   Ahh yes, man in his existence
Alas, so he be
    So be what?
        To see—
            the wonder of God's creation
        To feel—
            the warmth of the sun, the chill
            of the rain
        To sense—
            the awe of knowing
That be my joy!
Your joy I feel—it seems so real!
    Aye!   Indeed you know
        To cry—
            and be consoled
        To love—
            and be loved
        To die—
            to live with God
Go on, Go on—You have life
    To Be—A warm being, and oh so vital.

Blairanne Hoover Revak

His *Creed of Unbeing* was written by David and given to me while we were dating. I responded with my *Creed of Being*. They were both published in the Susquehanna University Publication of Student Writings our Senior year, 1965.

Made in the USA
Lexington, KY
07 January 2017